I Live, No Longer I

I Live, No Longer I

Paul's Spirituality of Suffering, Transformation, and Joy

Laura Reece Hogan

Foreword by Donald Senior, CP

Preface by Ruth Burrows, OCD

WIPF & STOCK · Eugene, Oregon

I LIVE, NO LONGER I
Paul's Spirituality of Suffering, Transformation, and Joy

Wipf & Stock
An Imprint of Wipf and Stock Publishers
199 W. 8th Ave., Suite 3
Eugene, OR 97401

www.wipfandstock.com

PAPERBACK ISBN: 978-1-5326-0107-1
HARDCOVER ISBN: 978-1-5326-0109-5
EBOOK ISBN: 978-1-5326-0108-8

Manufactured in the U.S.A.   JANUARY 9, 2017

To all the little birds, now and to come.
May you keep your eyes on what is above,
sing your song to God and all his creation,
and be a mighty warrior of the heart.

I have been crucified with Christ; yet I live, no longer I, but Christ lives in me; insofar as I now live in the flesh, I live by faith in the Son of God who has loved me and given himself up for me.

GALATIANS 2:19–20

We know that all things work for good for those who love God, who are called according to his purpose.

ROMANS 8:28

Just one thing: forgetting what lies behind but straining forward to what lies ahead, I continue my pursuit toward the goal, the prize of God's upward calling, in Christ Jesus.

PHILIPPIANS 3:13–14

Contents

Foreword

Donald Senior, CP

FOR MANY YEARS I have had the privilege of serving as the New Testament book review editor for *The Bible Today*, a journal that appears six times a year and focuses exclusively on biblical topics. The review articles I compose consist of brief evaluations of some twenty new books for each issue. Every time the deadline approaches to write my round-up of reviews, I worry that there might not be enough good books for the review article. I have always worried in vain. The production of books on the Bible and specifically the New Testament never seems to falter.

A heavy portion of these new publications focuses on the Pauline writings. The list of new titles over the years charts the prevailing interests of modern biblical scholarship. As a result, the majority of publications deal with historical, literary, and doctrinal issues triggered by Paul's letters. More traditional, historically inclined studies, for example, take up such issues as what we can know about Paul's biography: When and where was he born? What is the chronological sequence of the various letters he wrote? Under what circumstances did he write his letters? Was he a Roman citizen, as the Acts of the Apostles claims? And, if so, how did he gain such citizenship? What influence did his apparent origin in Tarsus, a Greco-Roman university town at the time, have on Paul? What was the nature of his training as a Pharisee and interpreter of the Law? And how should we track Paul's various missionary journeys? How many miles did Paul and his companions travel? And how did Paul meet his death? Was it during his house imprisonment in Rome as narrated in the conclusion to the Acts of the Apostles? Or was Paul eventually released from prison and was able to travel to Spain as he longed to do? A more recent focus on these and other basic historical questions is the issue of the historical reliability of the Acts of the Apostles, with most scholars preferring to give more weight to Paul's own testimony in his letters when the chronology and events narrated about Paul in Acts seem to differ from the description in Paul's own writings.

To these more traditional historical inquiries has been added in more recent years a focus on literary analysis of Paul's letters. To what degree do the Pauline letters follow the canons of ancient letter writing and how do they differ? Did Paul write these letters or dictate them? What are the thought structures of individual letters? How much was Paul influenced by the norms of ancient rhetoric in his writings? Are some of Paul's letters now present in the New Testament actually combinations of more than one letter, such as is often presumed with Paul's Second Letter to the Corinthians? What elements of Paul's letters are quotations from preexisting creedal formulas or early Christian hymns? And a perennially debated issue—are all of the letters attributed to Paul actually written by him or by later writers evoking his name? Here the focus is on the Pastoral Letters and Colossians and Ephesians.

Doctrinal or theological concerns also command a large portion of current publications on Paul. Topics such as what is the significance of Paul's "conversion" experience—and is it, in fact, accurately described as a "conversion" or, as Paul seems to label it in Galatians 1:15, a "call" situated within the broader framework of his Jewish heritage? Of course, an abiding doctrinal question is the centrality of the notion of "justification by faith alone" as being the heart of Paul's theological message—a perspective maintained strongly by traditional Protestant interpretation but now questioned by others who see it as one among many central themes in Paul's repertoire. And this issue, in turn, raises the question of Paul's view of the Jewish Law and its validity in the face of the Christ event. To what degree, in fact, is Paul's theology influenced by Jewish tradition? Does he have anything in common with the sectarian Jewish community at Qumran that was behind the Dead Sea Scrolls, a Jewish stream of tradition virtually contemporary with Paul? And is there also influence coming from Greco-Roman religions and moral philosophy? Barrels of ink have been employed on particular theological or ethical issues in Paul: his Christology, his ethics, his use of tradition, his ecclesiology, his view of sexuality, his eschatology, etc. An important underlying question here, too, is to what degree did Paul create Christian doctrine as distinct from being the recipient and interpreter of it? Should Paul be considered as, in fact, the true "founder" of Christianity?

To what degree was Paul and his theology shaped by the teachings and example of Christ?

More recent scholarship has been engaged in the question of a "new perspective" on Paul. Triggered by the writings of such great scholars as Krister Stendahl and Ed Sanders, a prevailing question has to do with Paul's relationship to Judaism. A more traditional view that saw a sharp cleavage between the Christian Paul and his life in Judaism has been called into question. Did Paul, in fact, reject his Jewish heritage in the wake of his encounter with Christ? Or, as Krister Stendahl had observed, was Paul's inaugural experience to be understood as a "call" or new vocation within the stream of his Jewish experience triggered by his faith in Christ as the promised Messiah of Israel. In this view Paul's mission to the Gentiles was not a rejection of his Jewish heritage but an expansion in his realization of God's plan for the salvation of the world. Sanders and others have also called for a rehabilitation of Christian understanding of ancient—and modern—Judaism—a call fueled in part by the tragedy of the Holocaust. Judaism is not to be thought of as a legalistic religion with its burdens of guilt and minute casuistry as it is often caricatured, but rather, in Sander's phrase, as a religion of "covenantal nomism"—that is, observance of the Jewish law was a faithful response to God's gift or grace of the Covenant. In Sander's view, Paul did not differ from Judaism because it was legalistic, as some have presumed, but because of Paul's view that Christ was the promised Messiah and Son of God—a view not shared by his contemporary Jewish peers.

This is a far from complete scan of recent scholarship but it does illustrate the kind of questions that most scholars have posed when turning to the Pauline letters. Against that backdrop, the graceful and inspiring work of Laura Reece Hogan takes a different path. Most of the prevailing scholarship on Paul is focused on understanding what Paul meant in his writings and how his original audiences might have understood them. The focus of this work, by contrast, is on what Paul's theology means *now*. While drawing on much of this accumulated Pauline scholarship, Laura's interest is in the meaning of Paul's theology for contemporary Christian spirituality and life. The spirit of this book reflects the call of Pope Benedict XVI in his exhortation, *Verbum Domini,* on the role of Scripture within the life and ministry of the Church. While endorsing the focus of modern biblical scholarship on historical criticism and allied methods, he also encouraged Catholic biblical scholars to explore the meaning of the Scriptures for the life of faith. Certainly most interpreters of Paul—past and present—recognize that the death and resurrection of Jesus stands at the heart of Paul's vision of Christian life and is at the core of his theology. Yet a smaller circle of Pauline interpreters deals in depth with the issue of the significance of Paul's theology of the cross on the essential dynamics of modern Christian life. Here is where Laura concentrates her attention.

A key existential question is the path into her reflections on Paul: "how do the inevitable suffering, loss, and death we experience interconnect with life and the divine?" (p. 2). Drawing in particular on Paul's fundamental and profound articulation of his Christology in the famous hymn quoted in his letter to the Philippians 2:5–11, Laura summarizes Paul's spirituality in the form of three fundamental dynamics found in the life of Jesus himself, in Paul as an ardent follower of Jesus, and as the pattern for the life of the Christian disciple and the community formed in Christ's name. Those three moments are: 1) *Kenosis,* or "self-emptying" exemplified in Christ's self-transcending love that leads to the cross and shapes its fundamental meaning; 2) *Enosis,* or "being with us"—the realization of God's abiding and sustaining presence even in the midst of suffering that Jesus himself experienced in his anguish on the cross; and 3) *Theosis,* or communion with the divine that was the essence of Jesus' existence and becomes the goal and fundamental hope of all human existence. Equally important, these dimensions of the Christ life lead to authentic joy and this is one of the major focuses of Laura's work. Finding profound and abiding joy in the midst of, and even through, suffering in the spirit of Christ is paradoxically the characteristic virtue of authentic Christian life.

Drawing on proven scholarship, Laura elaborates these fundamental dynamics or dimensions of the Christian life as found in Paul and offered to the Christian. She is not content simply with articulating this rich theology—a worthy task in itself—but also to tie it into Christian experience. She has been strongly influenced by Carmelite spirituality in her own life and several exemplars of that great tradition demonstrate her thesis, none more eloquently than Thérèse of Lisieux, the "little bird" who learned to soar like an eagle as she lived the very theology Laura describes. And with an example that might surprise and inspire many contemporary Christians, she probes the experience of Steven Colbert, famed comedian and now host of *The Late Show.* A devout Catholic, Colbert speaks movingly of eventually discovering in the tragic loss of his father and two brothers in a plane crash, not only acceptance of this intense suffering but, paradoxically, finding in this wrenching experience the reality of God's sustaining grace and the joy that flows from seeing all life as a gift. Amazing as it may be, Paul's passionate claim that "Christ lives in me" is echoed in the lives of Christians two thousand years later who find life in the midst of great suffering—the very heart of the Paschal mystery.

The first major statement of Pope Francis was his exhortation following the 2010 synod on Evangelization entitled "The Joy of the Gospel." Here, too, is found, as in Paul's life and teaching, this sure conviction that the heart of Christian spirituality is found in a personal and abiding relationship with Jesus—a portrayal of the Christian life expressed not only in the Pope's words but in his radiant joy, his love for the poor, his commitment to justice, and his prophetic courage.

Readers of Laura Reece Hogan's work whose title reveals its fundamental thesis—*I Live, No Longer I: Paul's Spirituality of Suffering, Transformation, and Joy*—will find the same depth of understanding, the same eloquent and inspiring language, and the same profound grasp of the biblical message. Those who want to find the heart of Paul's dynamic spirituality and meaning for our own lives of suffering and joy can turn to the pages of this beautiful book.

Preface

Ruth Burrows, OCD

THIS IS A WORK of light and love and of deep conviction. For all its simple, homely tone it is scholarly. The author has laboured long to acquire her easy familiarity with the Letters of Paul. Insight such as hers can come only from very prayerful exposure to the sacred word and, most importantly, the struggle to live its truth. The Holy Spirit prompts, guides and crowns with wisdom so earnest an endeavour to grow in the knowledge of Christ.

What gripped and absorbed our author's attention was St. Paul's discovery that the "cross of Christ," to him an insufferable anathema, was in fact, God's all-sufficient, effective answer to humankind's immeasurable woe: "if 'even death on a cross' had the supreme ability to restore and transform humanity, then that changed everything" (p. 2). "We must glory in the Cross of Our Lord Jesus Christ in whom is our salvation, life and resurrection: through whom we have been saved and set free" (an expansion of Gal 6:14 used as the Entrance chant to the Mass of the Lord's Supper). It seems to me that this triumphant song expresses Paul's teaching in a nutshell and *I Live, No Longer I,* echoes his voice in a splendid commentary bringing Paul's theology into the hearth and home of "little ones," of us, "ordinary folk." But of course, St. Paul himself was addressing "ordinary folk" of the time.

It is of passionate concern for Laura that many good, faithful Christians miss so much grace. They suffer their quota of human ills and yet—so it seems—fail to see them in the light of the saving Cross of Christ, so they hinder if not thwart God's desire to purify and transform them through their very pain. Generally speaking, we do not reflect sufficiently on the reality of our divine destiny. We are called to a destiny that far exceeds our insatiable thirst for perfect happiness and yet, though created for this bliss, we cannot, of ourselves attain it. Only God can bring us to it by "the immeasurable greatness of his power" at work in us (cf. Eph 1:19), the same mighty power by which he raised Christ from the dead and crowned him with glory and honour. We fail to appreciate the fact that the resurrection of the crucified Son of God who "emptied himself" (Phil 2:7) effected a cosmic shift in human existence; an absolutely new creation came to be. As Christians we are of that new creation, already in essence children of God, already sharing the divine nature. But do we really, consistently, live as such? Our author is passionately concerned to inform and to convince us of this new existence that faith in the Cross of Christ is offering us, opening up new horizons of hope and joyful possibility. What makes a truly Christian view of life completely different from, and even opposed to the natural world view, is the redemptive, transforming power of the Cross.

The very epitome of human woe hung on the cross on Good Friday, consumed with pain: physical torture, spiritual agony; humiliated, derided, seemingly defeated—the crucified Son of God! "God raised him high," we sing, and "gave him a name above every name" and he became in deed "our life our salvation and our resurrection." Everything depends on our truly believing this, and *choosing* to "live by faith in the Son of God who loved me and delivered himself for me" (Gal 2:20). Blessed we are to be given this insight and shown its implications for our daily living!

St. Paul urged his converts to see the world and the whole of human existence through the lens of faith; to judge everything, every event from the viewpoint of Christ, and Laura Hogan speaks with his voice today. She gives us poignant examples of fellow-travellers bravely struggling to maintain this faith-view in great pain of one kind or another. We readily appreciate the divinely-infused heroism displayed in these instances of grievous sufferings. Yet let us not overlook the almost constant demands on our faith-vision by our "pathetic," intimately personal little miseries: the wear and tear of our daily life, with its fatigues, its tedium; our temperamental moods and wounded sensitivities, our heartaches and disappointments; and the incommunicable pain of just being the person I am. We are ashamed to dignify all this as "suffering" and we assume implicitly that it has nothing to do with the Cross of Christ. In fact *it has everything to do with the Cross* and the more so perhaps because inglorious. Resolutely to believe that all the ills and afflictions of our human state are "the chalice which my Father has given me" and then, in union with Jesus, drinking it to the dregs is precisely sharing the death of Jesus so as to share his resurrection. It is a continual, habitual "no" to our natural egotism and a "yes" to Jesus. The Father is free to purify and transform us until "I live, no longer I, Christ lives in me." These afflictions will be with us anyway, exploited or not, how tragic to waste them.

I Live, No Longer I could change our lives but only if we accept the challenge and choose the "mind of Christ" over our own natural egotistical mind. Even the bitterest grief would be shot through with joy, "My joy"—Jesus' joy, deriving from certainty in the unshakeable, all-embracing, utterly tender and compassionate love of our Father.

Ruth Burrows
Carmel Quidenham

Acknowledgments

THIS BOOK IS A honeycomb created through long and intricate beework. It began with carefully researched and developed academic ideas, which pollinated principles in my daily living, and grew into a difficult writing process of capturing involved theological concepts in metaphor, example, and images of ordinary life. So it is not surprising that I have many people to acknowledge!

First and foremost, I thank Dr. Michael Downey, who has been a wonderful support and champion of this work, from beginning to finish. I am also grateful to Matthew Wimer, Brian Palmer, and Jana Wipf of Wipf & Stock for their kind assistance.

In addition to Dr. Downey, I thank Fr. J. Patrick Mullen, Fr. John P. Brennan, SMA, and Fr. Luke Dysinger, OSB, for their guidance and support of my Master's thesis, which provided the seeds for this book.

I am deeply grateful to those who have read, encouraged, and otherwise supported this book over the last several years: Fr. Donald Senior, CP, Sr. Ruth Burrows, OCD, Kate Smirnoff, Dr. Patrick Nichelson, Ann Evans, Debbie Gordon, Sr. Mary Leanne Hubbard, SND, Sr. Mary Glennon, CHF, Sr. Mary Grace Melcher, OCD, Jan McGuire, Olga Hayek, Dr. Susan Rose, Martha Mareno, Elizabeth Walker, Sr. Joyce Gaspardo, CSJ, Eileen Bonaduce, Laura Kaplan, Anne-Marie Reader, Stephanie Vassallo, Katrice Boland, Gretchen Ford, and Elizabeth Kuelbs. I would like to particularly acknowledge Karen Berman Riddle and Michelle Abend Bauman, dear friends who gave generously of themselves to help with this work.

I thank the members of my Lay Carmelite community, the Blessed Titus Brandsma Community, for their constant prayers and encouragement. I am deeply grateful to the communities of the Quidenham Carmelite Monastery, the Pewaukee Carmelite Monastery, and the Terre Haute Carmelite Monastery for their prayers and invaluable support.

I thank my loving family, who encouraged and supported me every step of the way—my husband Mike, and our three amazing children, Caitlin, Connor, and Amanda. Special gratitude goes to Caitlin, who provided impromptu and excellent editorial assistance.

This work would not exist without the love, unexpected gifts, and gentle guidance over the last ten years of the Lord. I am eternally grateful for the journey, and most of all, for the companionship.

Introduction

Paul in Prison

WHAT COULD POSSIBLY GENERATE constant joy in a person locked up in a brutal prison, all plans dashed, with death looming on the horizon? Paul of Tarsus, stuck squarely in the harsh captivity of a first-century prison, could not contain his excitement, and yes, his joy, in what he perceived all around him as evidence that God was at work. "I want you to know," he wrote to his fledgling community at Philippi, "that my situation has turned out rather to advance the gospel, so that my imprisonment has become well known in Christ throughout the whole praetorium and to all the rest, and so that the majority of the brothers, having taken encouragement in the Lord from my imprisonment, dare more than ever to proclaim the word fearlessly."[1] Paul interprets the fact of his imprisonment, and his suffering, as directly instrumental to furthering the spread of the gospel in a way both unexpected and effective. Moreover, he notes that the intention of these new preachers, whether springing from rivalry or love, is irrelevant, because either way Christ is proclaimed: "And in that I rejoice" (Phil 1:18). How much more would Paul have rejoiced if he had any idea that his sojourn in prison and his resulting short letter to the Philippians would be effective in yet another way—the letter would itself powerfully proclaim the word of God, would endure through centuries, would be published all over the world, would be examined in volumes upon volumes of scholarly work, and would speak to and inspire countless human hearts? It is hard to fully grasp the impact and effectiveness of Paul's time in prison. In fact, you yourself would not be reading these very words if Paul had not been imprisoned.

---

1. Phil 1:12. Unless otherwise noted, all quotations from the Bible utilize *New American Bible.*

Paul's experience of God's effectiveness even in situations which seemed radically lost and hopeless had its roots in the cross of Jesus Christ. Paul discovered that the cross of Jesus Christ had something to do with not just Jesus Christ, but Paul himself and all humanity. If "even death on a cross" (Phil 2:8) had the supreme ability to restore and transform humanity, then that changed everything. Everything must be reinterpreted through this powerful and paradoxical lens of the cross. Even the experience of prison takes on new meaning. Even prison, in all its misery and suffering, contains the power to accomplish the transformative will of God—prison represents not defeat but victory on a divine scale. Yet prison is not just for those languishing behind bars. Prison is a universal human experience. Ultimately, don't we all encounter a personal experience of prison, portable or otherwise?

Part of the human condition is colliding with pain, with things we do not control, with things we would change if we could. To me, one of the more profound questions is: how do the inevitable suffering, loss, and death we experience interconnect with life and the divine? As a Christian, I look to my faith for an answer, and specifically to the life and person of Jesus Christ. In pursuit, I spent years at a seminary pondering, praying, and researching this question, then developed, wrote, and defended a thesis about it, and then spent many years after that living out the sometimes challenging insights of my work. As an attorney, it comes naturally to me to ask questions, and to utilize reasoning and comprehensive research in developing responses. I am also a mother of three, so I have plenty of experience with the messiness, profound love, unpredictability, joy, sacrifice, and vulnerability which accompany daily life with my children. Additionally, as a professed Third Order Carmelite, I am a Catholic called more deeply by God into a life of contemplation drawing on Carmelite spirituality, which is fired by intimate transformative relationship with God. Most importantly, I am a human being, who, like you, encounters the mysterious twists and turns, and light and darkness of life every day.

So this hunt of mine to uncover some answers to my question has been an involved journey. It has wound and evolved through quiet libraries, simmering pots in my kitchen, sun-drenched orange groves at the seminary, soccer games and cross country meets of my children, sudden hurts, sudden joys, the silence of prayer, and the connections and tears of daily life. I have come to experience that one of the gifts of Jesus Christ is the way his life shows us that all aspects of our lives, even the dark and painful parts we would rather exclude or forget, are included and embraced by the divine. We are not alone in the dark places, and in fact God uses those dark places in mysterious ways for his unexpected and effective purposes. Moreover, Jesus has given us critical information about how to shift our perspective, how to see all the moments of our lives as points of relationship with God, and how to interconnect them in a transformative way. Paul the Apostle discovered this crucial pattern weaving through the person of Jesus, and made it a priority to teach it and live it out himself. After I became aware of this pattern through Paul's writings and began to implement a new way of experiencing the moments of my life, I found that this paradigm shift made a vast difference in not just my spiritual life, but in my whole life. I am writing this book for one purpose: I believe that these concepts, revealed by Jesus and articulated by Paul, are critical to living out the Christian life, and I want to share them with you. These hard-won treasures of wisdom and insight are meant to be handed on and lived out by all who want to grow into deeper relationship with the divine.

The concepts we will examine derive from a Christian context and framework, yet also reflect universal truths about the human condition. While the theological language and foundations employed here arise from the Catholic tradition for the simple reason that I myself am Catholic and received my theological training in a Catholic setting, the direct reliance on scripture hopefully makes this work accessible to those from all Christian denominations, and those coming from other faiths open to the ideas and scriptural underpinnings of Christianity. I do not see the ideas treated here as limited to an audience of those in the Christian tradition for the basic fact that suffering, transformation, and joy are fundamental to our humanity, and this book speaks directly to that universal experience.

In the years I have read and absorbed Paul, I have grown to deeply respect him not solely as the Apostle but also as a human being encountering Jesus Christ. It is sometimes easy to think of Paul as a distant biblical figure, far from the lives you and I live. Yet he was a human being struggling with loss and suffering also, just as you and I do, as all humans do as part of the human condition. I would like to challenge you as you read this to think of him as a human person encountering Jesus Christ. It is no more or less than the humanity of Paul that provides us with insight into the divine-human relationship. As a human being, Paul experienced Jesus as profoundly *with him*. The first message he gives to all of us is that, as human beings, we have been drawn into deep and transformative relationship with God.

Paul discovered and wanted to teach us that not only was the cross of Jesus Christ a paradox, but this very same paradox threads through the experience of all Christian life. Ironically what may seem to be death is paradoxically life, what may seem to be defeat is paradoxically victory, what may seem to be loss is paradoxically gain, and all Christian experience flows through this strange but powerful paradigm. Once we begin to perceive reality through this paradoxical lens of the cross, our ways of interpreting events and people in our lives change and expand—we begin to leave room for the perhaps hidden yet effective purposes of God in all things.

Paul came to construe the very life of Jesus Christ as a form or pattern of life. He found a marvelous and hidden shape in the life of Jesus, with contours of self-emptying, being with us, and divine unity. In the Letter to the Philippians he presents this pattern in the majestic "Christ Hymn" (Phil 2:6–11), so called because it is considered by many scholars to be a pre-existing liturgical hymn which Paul employed in his letter. In it, as we will explore in these pages, Paul describes Jesus in three moments of self-emptying or *kenosis*, being with us or *enosis*, and divine unity or *theosis*. But Paul didn't stop there. He realized something critical about the pattern he had observed in the life and person of Jesus Christ. He perceived that in the same way he was "no longer I, but Christ lives in me" (Gal 2:20), a parallel pattern was to be expressed in and through the life of Paul himself, and in and through the lives of all Christians pursuing "the goal, the prize of God's upward calling, in Christ Jesus" (Phil 3:14).

For Paul, this three-part understanding of the life and person of Jesus, and the corresponding lives of those who follow him, provided a fundamental key to understanding all Christian experience, and a critical lens of interpretation for all aspects of life. As he examined his own life through this lens, he became aware that God's operation in and through his life took on this pattern, a form observable not only in Paul's life story but also in individual moments of personal experience. As we take a look ourselves at these three moments and how they fit together, first in the life of Christ, then in the life of Paul, and in the lives of other followers of Christ, we also can detect what Paul did: that the life of Jesus itself provides a map of the divine "upward calling."

These three moments can be described as moments of relationship between God and us. As we will explore, God touches and transforms us and our lives in and through these three moments of divine-human inter-action. When God touches, God transforms. When we begin to perceive the touches of God in our lives, we also begin to perceive not only our own transformation, but also the infinite effectiveness of divine action, sometimes beyond the bounds of human expectation or understanding. This growing insight enables us to connect the dots between moments in our lives and the divine.

Paul knew the practical concerns of the people in his communities, and so in offering this pattern to them, he also offered himself and others as examples of ways the Christ pattern could be played out. An integral part of the example was not only the outward behavior of an individual, but the interior development of the person—her thoughts and prayer. We will investigate some of what Paul intended to be included in the concept of example modeled on the Christ pattern. As we ourselves consider ways in which we echo and reflect this pattern, we begin to recognize that the interior life shapes and fires the exterior aspect of our lives, and the exterior experience is brought back in to reshape and fire the interior.

But all this is hardly just about the individual's spiritual development. Paul was keenly aware of the part the single individual or community played in the transmission of the gospel. Paul wrote to the community at Thessalonica, "And you became imitators of us and of the Lord, receiving the word in great affliction, with joy from the holy Spirit, so that you became a model for all the believers in Macedonia and in Achaia" (1 Thess 1:6–7). Paul perceived individual transformation as part of a larger picture, as part of the transmission of the word of God, and part of the divine work in the world. We will examine what Paul meant by this and how we also play our part in this great circular model of divine revelation.

This participation in the transformative work of God was not some kind of mechanical exercise for Paul. Living in and through Christ became not only his life but his joy. In fact, Paul's use of joy in his letters becomes almost a signpost, an instruction to us about how to interpret events and people in our lives. We will consider Paul's joy and what it says to us about how to value and discern. In particular, we will listen to what Paul has to say to us about taking joy in our real and constant relationship with God, joy in our fulfillment of purpose in and through God, and joy in detecting the effectiveness of God's ongoing work in our own hearts and lives, in the hearts and lives of others, and in human history.

Living our lives and simply being human sometimes involves suffering, whether it stems from physical, emotional, psychological or spiritual pain or loss, whether experienced by ourselves or by those whom we love.

When we are in the excruciating midst of pain and loss, we have a very hard time thinking of anything except when and how the pain will stop. Paul grasped that the cross of Jesus Christ offered a radically new way to perceive and experience suffering. As the founder of communities encountering suffering in many forms, including death, Paul came to realize that his most urgent pastoral task was to teach his people to shift their perspective, to perceive divine effectiveness, to experience a new unity with Jesus Christ in and through all aspects of their lives, even suffering. Today, Paul's insights remain just as important and life-altering, whether our challenges and sufferings take place in everyday or extreme circumstances. Human suffering takes on so many faces, and human history has so many permutations of pain. Yet the wisdom in Paul's insights remains vitally relevant to Christian lives today, in the midst of whatever prison we find ourselves.

In 1994, I made a day retreat at the top of a California mountain with my sponsor Jane a few weeks before I was received into the church. The task before us as we sat in the sunshine was to read and contemplate a scripture passage. Jane read it out loud to me, and when she came to the words, "signs will come from the sky" (Luke 21:11), a gigantic red-tailed hawk came rushing down behind me, and I heard the swooshing beat of its wings just before it brushed heavily across the top of my head, then shot back upward into the sky again. Jane and I stared at each other in awe. It seemed significant, magnificent, strange and yet also part of our mountain landscape, our scripture, our ordinary lives. I was touched by all of those elements, and I was never the same. I hope that the message of this book will touch you the same way that hawk came to me—something strikingly beautiful, significant, and mysterious coming from beyond, yet something speaking directly and powerfully into your ordinary lived experience. That improbable and electric intersection of something divine from beyond and something human here in everyday life, and the love it reveals, forms the basis of the message of Jesus as told by Paul.

Chapter 1

De-Centering and Divine Presence

WHAT DOES IT MEAN to not be the center of one's own life? After all, we are embodied human beings, firmly and concretely rooted within our physical frame, thinking with our own brain, feeling with our own heart, sensing with our own senses, perceiving and interpreting our own experience. Yet we are exquisitely intertwined with others from the moment we come to exist as a human being. Much of what we experience as life is the ebb and flow of relationship—with ourselves, with other human beings, and with the divine. If you think about it, you can probably link every moment of your life to one or more of these relationships. These three relationships form the core of not simply life, but also life lived in accordance with the greatest commandment: "You shall love the Lord, your God, with all your heart, with all your being, with all your strength, and with all your mind, and your neighbor as yourself."[1] You are to love God, your neighbor, and yourself. The theological trick of this threesome is that if you truly and radically love each of these three, the lines dividing the three begin to blur. When the loved self becomes fundamentally reoriented in love toward God and neighbor, the self necessarily shifts and de-centers.

This concept of de-centering absolutely does not mean becoming a doormat to the world or to anyone. It does not mean forgetting to love ourselves along the way. But it does mean expanding our love and our hearts to the breaking point, at which point our divine partner in love steps in to help. It does mean realizing your greatest potential as a human person. It does mean deep and intense participation in a love much bigger than ourselves. It means participation in the divine life.

1. Luke 10:27; cf. Matt 22:37–40; Mark 12:29–31.

This radical shift happened in Paul. His encounter with the risen Jesus Christ on the road to Damascus literally knocked him to the ground and re-engineered his sight. In that moment he went from Saul, a man determined to persecute and destroy the followers of Jesus, to a man stripped of his footing, purpose, and vision.

> On his journey, as he was nearing Damascus, a light from the sky suddenly flashed around him. He fell to the ground and heard a voice saying to him, "Saul, Saul, why are you persecuting me?" He said, "Who are you, sir?" The reply came, "I am Jesus, whom you are persecuting. Now get up and go into the city and you will be told what you must do." The men who were traveling with him stood speechless, for they heard the voice but could see no one. Saul got up from the ground, but when he opened his eyes he could see nothing; so they led him by the hand and brought him to Damascus. For three days he was unable to see, and he neither ate nor drank.[2]

An account of this experience is given three times by the author of Acts, each time as describing the pivotal moment of Paul's conversion.[3] Yet all was not accomplished in Paul in that moment. It took time for Paul to fully work through the meaning of Jesus Christ and his cross and how his new orientation to Christ was to be lived.

You may not have been thrown to the ground by a blinding light, but you probably have experienced moments of de-centering. Have you ever realized that you would change your schedule, your plans, or even your life's ambition because of love? After the birth of my first child, I remember saying to my husband that I was waiting for my life to return to normal. But what took time for me to realize was that I had a new normal. I was no longer a practicing attorney showing up at an office and immersing my mind in legal problems. I was a new mother who, blessed with such an option, had chosen to stay at home with her baby. When I looked at my tiny daughter, my heart wanted to overflow love into her. I wanted to hold her, feed her, change her diapers, read to her, sing and talk to her, and wake up in the middle of the night for her. I counted all that as pure joy, and it was. I had been fundamentally de-centered by the love of another.

---

2. Acts 9:3–8. Saul was his Semitic name, Paul was his Greco-Roman name. There is a shift from the use of Saul to Paul in Acts 13:9.

3. Acts 9, 22, and 26.

This type of de-centering takes place within us on a much more profound level when we feel love for the divine awake within us. When we experience that we are deeply loved, and that we can love in return, we are forever changed. We are no longer the person we once were, with the concerns and goals of an individual untouched by another. We are radically converted into a person empowered and charged by relationship. We share the sufferings, goals, and joys of the one we love, God, and our neighbor, be it spouse, child, parent, friend, teacher, pupil, caregiver, patient, and so on. The parent-child relationship serves as an excellent example of shared concerns. What parent doesn't suffer along with their child undergoing bullying, sickness, loss, or even death? What parent doesn't feel the satisfaction of their child when she gives her balloon to the girl who just lost hers to the wind? What parent doesn't share the joy of their child when they learn to tie their shoelaces, master the violin, or graduate from college? The divine relationship is perhaps less tangible, but no less intense an experience of union; in fact, it is much more intense. Teresa of Avila, a sixteenth-century Carmelite saint, described her experience of spiritual union with Jesus Christ as a total exchange of cares: in a vision Christ "told her that it was time she took upon her His affairs as if they were her own and that He would take her affairs upon Himself."[4]

Paul undoubtedly became de-centered in his moment of conversion, yet something else happened after that initial encounter on the road to Damascus. The totality of the experience of de-centering came in and through subsequent experiences of love. In the years that followed his conversion, Paul's writings attest to a developing relationship with Jesus Christ, an overwhelmingly intimate, loving, and growing relationship. The letters which Paul wrote to his emergent communities overflow with this love for, in, and through Jesus Christ. But Paul's words reflect more than a simple affection of the heart. The text aches for deep union with the divine, for an entanglement so profound that the two are one in all things, in sorrow and in joy, in death and in life. Paul's new sense of self connected so closely with his experience of the crucified Christ that he wrote to the Galatians: "I have been crucified with Christ; yet I live, no longer I, but Christ lives in me; insofar as I now live in the flesh, I live by faith in the Son of God who has loved me and given himself up for me."[5] Paul's experience and expression of

4. Teresa of Avila, *Interior Castle* (Peers) 212–213; see also Teresa of Avila, *Interior Castle* (Kavanaugh) 433.

5. Gal 2:19–20; cf. 1 Cor 2:2; Rom 6:6, 8.

de-centered identity in his letters arises not only from his loving relation-ship with Jesus Christ, but also his understanding of the meaning of the cross.

Paul wanted his communities to know about this drastic de-centering experience.[6] He desired the people in his communities to experience the love of Jesus Christ in the same de-centering way. So he goes to great lengths to describe his own experience. The Letter to the Philippians provides an excellent example of his effort to communicate the experience of becoming de-centered through relationship with Jesus Christ. In Philippians, Paul makes a point of contrasting his former life as a Pharisee with his current life in Christ (Phil 3:5–9). Whereas Paul before had "grounds for confidence even in the flesh" (3:4) given his status as a Pharisee, he now in contrast does not put his confidence in flesh, but in the spirit of God and Jesus Christ (3:3). Paul's language also points to the totality of his experience of transforma-tion in Christ—he considers "everything" a loss, he has accepted "the loss of all things" (3:8); in contrast the good of knowing the Lord Jesus Christ is "supreme" or "surpassing" (3:8), his only objective is to "gain Christ and be found in him" (3:8–9). We can detect Paul's own awareness of his fundamen-tal shift in perspective regarding what is of value. He considers all the things of his past "so much rubbish" in comparison with the "supreme good" and "gain" of Christ (3:8). Finally, Paul reveals in this passage a clear reorientation of self to Christ: he accepts the loss of all things in favor of knowing Christ (3:8), he wishes to "gain Christ and to be found in him" (3:8–9), and he de-pends upon Christ for such fundamental elements as righteousness (3:9) and resurrection (3:10–11). In particular, Paul indicates the method by which he will attain Christ and the resurrection: through the "sharing of his sufferings" and "being conformed" to the death of Christ (3:10). Paul discloses that not only has his sense of self shifted toward Christ, but his fundamental identity is centered on participation in the life of Christ.

So we can identify at least some of the characteristics of Paul's shift in sense of self: he has moved from confidence in the flesh to confidence in the spirit; the experience of transformation in Christ has impacted all things in Paul's life and been total; Paul is aware of this fundamental shift in his per-spective regarding what is of value; and not only is Paul's identity reoriented to Christ, but he sees himself as participating in the life of Christ. Yet all we have examined so far does not adequately convey the depth of Paul's sense of intimate participation and union with Jesus Christ. For it is this element

6. Fowl, "Who's Characterizing Whom," 537–553; 545, 550.

which truly characterizes the post-Damascus Paul, a Paul in love with and loved by Jesus Christ to such a degree that it is no longer simply Paul, but Paul found in Christ (Phil 3:9) and Christ in possession of Paul (Phil 3:12), Paul magnifying Christ either in life or in death (Phil 1:20), Paul spiritually at one with the crucified Christ, "yet I live, no longer I, but Christ lives in me." Paul's identity has been simultaneously electrified and blurred in this all-consuming, de-centering, disintegrating yet joyful transformation from Paul's "I" to a putative "we."

We can surmise that for Paul, the blinding light of Damascus cleared the way for a new and eternal creation within him. But Paul knew that de-centering of self was not an experience for him alone, but for all. He realized that it was an essential component of experience for each member of his communities. If you were going to plant a garden, what would you do first? You would clear the ground of all the weeds and grass before you began planting your new and ordered seeds. Paul had a specific idea of what the garden ought to look like, his own garden, the individual Christian's garden, and their belonging to the wider garden of Christ, and he knew that self-centeredness and fear were weeds that would choke it. Paul also knew the identity of the gardener: "For God is the one who, for his good purpose, works in you both to desire and to work" (Phil 2:13). Paul repeatedly stresses the importance of this de-centering of self in favor of Christ and others as the clearing prerequisite to the Christian life, and the transformative work of the Gardener.

You might be thinking, "That's all good and fine for Paul. Paul was a mystic. Paul had visions of Jesus Christ and spoke with him. He was transformed by him. How do I do that? How does that apply to me today? After all, I do my best, but I am not exactly getting caught up to the third heaven like Paul or levitating like Teresa of Avila."

Paul indeed was a mystic.[7] He alone among the apostles knew Jesus Christ entirely through mystical experience, after his death and resurrection.[8] Scripture provides powerful evidence that Paul's vivid relationship with Jesus Christ flowed from mystical encounter and prayer. In our reference to mysticism here and elsewhere we refer to a state of heightened consciousness of connection or union with the transcendent reality of God which arises either within the bounds, or surpassing the bounds, of

---

7. Specifically, Paul was "a first-century Jewish apocalypticist, and as such, he was also a mystic." Segal, *Paul the Convert*, 34.

8. Murphy-O'Connor, *Paul: His Story,* 23–24; McGinn, *Foundations of Mysticism*, 70.

ordinary experience. The conversion experience on the road to Damascus (Acts 9:3–9; 22:6–10; 26:12–19), Paul's description of his interaction regarding the mysterious "thorn in the flesh" (2 Cor 12:7–9), the experience of "being caught up in the third heaven" (2 Cor 12:1–5), other ecstatic visions (Acts 16:9; 18:9; 22:17–21; Gal 1:11–12; 2:2), as well as his call to constant prayer (e.g., 1 Thess 5:17) provide some hints as to Paul's mysticism and corresponding vision. Mystic "vision" implies two elements: (1) perception of a reality belonging to the realm of God which is beyond that which we experience in the earthly existence; and (2) the ability to articulate, interpret and transmit that vision to others. The gift of sight demands to be shared for the good of those who still cannot see; the one with vision must return from the mystical experience or life to guide others.[9] Yet the mystic necessarily has a foot in both worlds as witness, translator, and example.

Paul makes a point of the mystical source of his proclamation in his letter to the Galatians: "Now I want you to know, brothers, that the gospel preached by me is not of human origin. For I did not receive it from a human being, nor was I taught it, but it came through a revelation of Jesus Christ" (Gal 1:11–12). The revelation was specifically to be shared and proclaimed: God "was pleased to reveal his Son to me, so that I might proclaim him to the Gentiles" (Gal 1:16). Thus Paul himself describes his mystical and singular experience of the heavenly—Jesus Christ—while still anchored in the earthly, a mystical experience given for the purpose of proclamation. The dual heavenly-earthly perception of the mystic both informs and fires the proclamation.

However, did you notice our definition of mysticism? Mysticism is a state of heightened consciousness of connection or union with the transcendent reality of God which arises *either within the bounds, or surpassing the bounds, of ordinary experience*. The extraordinary mysticism of Paul, or of Teresa of Avila, is not the only experience of mysticism. The original sense of the word *mysterion* as used by the earliest Christian writers implied a deeply felt sense of God's mysteries. It was only later, first in the emphasis upon ecstasies found in the work of Augustine (354–430), and later in the writings of Bernard of Clairvaux (1090–1153), Henry Suso (c. 1300–1366), and ultimately Teresa of Avila (1515–1582), that mysticism was considered increasingly more personal, affective, and psychological,

---

9. This paradigm figures in Plato's "Allegory of the Cave," found in book 7 of *Republic*, which set a pattern observable in subsequent interpretations by Christian mystics. McGinn, *Foundations of Mysticism*, 29.

with extraordinary features of visions, locutions, raptures, levitations, and similar supernatural phenomena.[10] One author notes that this emphasis over the years gave rise to a sense that "Christian mysticism is something extraordinary, reserved for a chosen few."[11] But that changed in the twentieth century, when a debate arose among theologians regarding Thérèse of Lisieux (1873–1897), a nineteenth-century Carmelite saint who never experienced extraordinary mystical phenomena yet clearly had an intense experience of the presence of God in her ordinary life. Was she a mystic? On the one hand, some argued, she could not be considered a mystic because of the lack of such extraordinary mystical phenomena. But on the other hand, what was true mysticism anyway? Theologian Karl Rahner (1904–1984) brought the sense of the term back closer to its original meaning. In addition to the more extraordinary forms of mysticism, Rahner concluded that mysticism must also include "everyday mysticism" which plays out in a heightened awareness or consciousness of God.[12]

That everyday mysticism includes you and me, even in the ordinariness of our everyday lives, if we pay attention. In her autobiography, Thérèse of Lisieux described herself and her relationship with God in a lovely metaphor. She was a little bird, she explained, a bird both small and flightless. She longed to be a powerful eagle that could fly to the heavens, like the great saints and the angels, to be a mighty instrument of God. Nevertheless, she could only be what she was, a little bird unable to fly, prone to get distracted or even fall asleep, and totally dependent on the love and mercy of God. Yet she dared to look to heaven and desire to attain to, and mightily serve, her God.[13] Thérèse arrived at the conclusion that God would not give her such a burning desire if he did not mean to satisfy it. She decided that she could attain to her goal even in her ordinary life: she would give all her love, even in the smallest of things.[14] This "little way" of Thérèse speaks to our relationship with God in our everyday lives. Even the smallest of birds can still gaze into the heavens.

Not only can the smallest birds gaze, they can perceive and communicate what they perceive to others. That is mystic vision. Ordinary events,

10. See Wiseman, "Mysticism," 682–687.

11. Ibid., 687.

12. Ibid., 688.

13. Thérèse of Lisieux, *Story of a Soul* (Clarke), 198–200; Thérèse of Lisieux, *The Story of a Soul* (Edmonson), 221–225.

14. Thérèse of Lisieux, *Story of a Soul* (Clarke), 194–197; Thérèse of Lisieux, *The Story of a Soul* (Edmonson), 217–221.

ordinary interactions with people, ordinary prayer experiences contain powerful connections with the divine, if we are able to perceive the presence of the divine. In fact, true mystic vision is readily available to us, if we attend to the lenses provided to us, lenses which are sometimes hidden but highly effective—specifically, the lenses furnished by the person and life of Jesus Christ. The little bird may stay on the ground, but has eyes to see the heavens. Just as we described Paul's vision as "dual" because he simultaneously could perceive both the earthly reality and the heavenly reality, so our little bird may also have this type of dual perception. She may experience the reality of her earthly existence—capturing a worm, getting wet in the rain—yet she simultaneously has her heart and gaze set on heaven—glimpsing the eagles as they soar, feeling the sun on her wings.[15] Like Paul, she also has a little bird foot in both realities, and she knows and feels them both.

Paul realized that an awareness of these two sometimes competing and conflicting realities provided his burgeoning communities with a key tool for reinterpreting their experience of persecution and suffering. By worldly standards, being a first-century Christian seemed like a bad idea. After all, you were very likely to be ostracized, misunderstood, imprisoned, or even killed. Yet for these Christians, the governing concern stemmed not from the world, but from heaven. Paul urged this shift in perspective, from the earthly to the heavenly.[16] In the Letter to the Philippians he specifically contrasts the concerns of those grounded in the earthly with the concerns of those focused upon the heavenly:

> For many, as I have often told you and now tell you even in tears, conduct themselves as enemies of the cross of Christ. Their end is destruction. Their God is their stomach; their glory is in their "shame." Their minds are occupied with earthly things. But our citizenship is in heaven, and from it we also await a savior, the Lord Jesus Christ.[17]

A shift in perspective from the earthly to the heavenly would enable a person to clearly and accurately perceive what was of value. That was Paul's

---

15. Thérèse of Lisieux, *Story of a Soul* (Clarke), 198–200.

16. We take this terminology from Paul's contrast of the earthly and heavenly found in Phil 3:19–20. Although Paul speaks elsewhere of flesh versus spirit (e.g., Rom 8:5–9; Gal 5:16–25; cf. Phil 3:3–4), the contrast Paul sets up in Philippians has to do with two conflicting realities which the Philippians experience as people who live in the world yet are citizens of heaven, which is our present concern.

17. Phil 3:18–20.

primary pastoral concern and prayer for his communities, that they shift away from reliance upon an earthly understanding of things, and toward an increasingly clearer God-centered vision: "And this is my prayer: that your love may increase ever more and more in knowledge and every kind of perception, to discern what is of value, so that you may be pure and blameless for the day of Christ, filled with the fruit of righteousness that comes through Jesus Christ for the glory and praise of God" (Phil 1:9–11).

Paul's insight remains relevant for us today. It is all too easy to interpret the pain and losses in our everyday lives from an earthly perspective; after all, it stabs, it leaves holes, it aches; sometimes the hurt is excruciating and overwhelming. But even as our wings get wet, as Thérèse might say, even as our hearts are drenched in misery and drowning in dark waters, we should remember to turn our eyes to the heavens. Simply by including the divine in our overall vision, we expand our horizon of interpretation. More significantly, as we make the life and person of Jesus Christ our primary lens, we automatically began to cultivate that heavenly vision by reconsidering all life experience through the paradox of the cross, a cross which seemed by all accounts to mean brutal death, yet as we explore in the next chapter, also signified salvation and new life.

In Paul's view the key to perceiving the heavenly perspective is holding fast to God and his promise to be with us even when the clouds are dark. Paul knew that sometimes when we are in the middle of a crisis or painful situation it can seem to us like God simply is not present there with us. In his letters Paul reassures us that "[t]he Lord is near" (Phil 4:5); he challenges us, "Do you not realize that Jesus Christ is in you?" (2 Cor 13:5). We have in the Gospel of Matthew the words of Jesus: "I am with you always, until the end of the age" (Matt 28:20). Paul built upon the frequent promise of God to be with us found in Hebrew scripture; for example in Isaiah: "When you pass through the water, I will be with you;/ in the rivers you shall not drown./ When you walk through fire, you shall not be burned;/ the flames shall not consume you" (Isa 43:2). As many have noted, God does not promise to prevent the flood or fire, but he does promise to be *with us* in the flood or fire. The uninterrupted presence of God with us in and through all things is a critical part of the vision of Paul, who declared: "What will separate us from the love of Christ? Will anguish, or distress, or persecution, or famine, or nakedness, or peril, or the sword? . . . No, in all these things we conquer overwhelmingly through him who loved us" (Rom 8:35, 37). For Paul, not only is God present with us, but God is at work for good in and through all things (Rom 8:28). Again, the promise is not prevention of difficulty or pain, but to be with us and bring us through situations with love.

Many years ago, my seven-year-old daughter woke up with a high fever at 6 am. She told me, "Mommy, my side hurts." Alarm bells went off in my head and everything slowed down in my sudden panic. The doctor on call told me that she was probably fine if she had not vomited, which she had not. But then she asked again where the pain was, and my little scientific daughter replied, "one inch below my bellybutton on the right side." The doctor told me to take her to the emergency room immediately.

As I rushed to get dressed to leave, interiorly a calm voice told me not to throw on just anything, but to dress for the day. I stopped, teetering between all-out panic and the peace of the communication. On the one hand, it frightened me that God might be suggesting that this day would be spent at the hospital. But the unmoved presence of the divine I felt was so reassuring that I simply dressed for the day. My daughter vomited on the drive to the hospital. She was admitted, and I helped her change into a little hospital gown covered in tigers. After various tests were performed, the ER doctors determined that she needed emergency surgery to remove her appendix. She was wheeled into surgery before noon.

That day was a very strange one in Southern California. It hailed violently off and on all day. The odd and sudden nature of the storm matched my inner turmoil as I waited anxiously for news of my little daughter. Finally a nurse told me the surgery was over, and I could see her, tiny and pale in a recovery room. I stayed with her the rest of the afternoon until my husband came to spend the night with her in the hospital, and I left to go home to our two younger children. As I came to the exit of the hospital, I was stopped short by the sight of pounding hail and the mounting piles of hailstones. I waited for a while for the storm to ease before I drove home. Almost as soon as I got home, the storm picked up again. As I stood before my kitchen window and gazed out at the relentless hailstones, I noticed a huge red-tailed hawk hanging in mid-air above our fence. I marveled at it—it was completely undaunted by the hurling hailstones and it seemed to float effortlessly on the wind of the storm. Then interiorly I heard: "I am the hawk in the hailstorm."

And it was true. Just like that magnificent hawk in the midst of the hailstorm, the Lord had been with me in my storm that day. The hail and wind had lashed in terrifying ways, but the presence of the Lord remained peacefully unmoved, even in the midst of the storm, with me. I will never forget watching the shape of that hawk as it lingered, I in my kitchen thankful for the health of my little girl in the hospital with tigers on her gown, and the peacefully hovering hawk punctuating the thrilling and joyful point that God was with me, even in my dark place.

Like Paul, when we come to focus our gaze on Jesus Christ, things shift. We no longer inhabit the center of our lives, but something brighter, more expansive, and more inclusive becomes the center. The divine steps in, and we begin to participate in the divine life. This de-centering process functions to open the way to a new way of living and perceiving. We take up a new set of lenses, all derived from the central lens of the cross. We take up different ways of looking at the world, people, and events which more accurately assign true value. We perceive the effective work and design of God, even and especially in the absence of extraordinary mystical phenomena. We become increasingly aware of the loving and constant presence of God with us, even in the hailstorms of our lives. We may be little birds, but we only have to pay attention to begin perceiving the pattern which has been left behind for us in scripture, a stunningly beautiful and accurate roadmap of the divine upward calling grounded in everyday experience of the divine presence. The pages that follow are devoted to uncovering this map and connecting its direction intimately to the moments of our lives.

Chapter 2

Perspective Adjustment, or the Paradox of the Cross

THE ENTIRE PLOT OF the middle-grade work of fiction entitled *Alcatraz Versus the Evil Librarians* centers on a struggle for a bag of sand.[1] Why is the bag of sand so significant? Because the Sands of Rashid hold the power to be smelted into lenses which, worn as eyeglasses, would reveal pivotal secrets in the battle between good and evil (well, between the Smedrys and the Evil Librarians anyway). In the story, skillfully crafted lenses provide the key to understanding the true state of things, and the Sands of Rashid will be made into the ultimate lenses for perceiving the most sought-after truths of the Librarian world.

The cross of Jesus Christ provides us with the ultimate and invaluable lens for perceiving the true state of things. Sometimes it may seem as inscrutable as the mysterious bag of sand in the story, yet it holds the greatest of power as a lens, and brings into focus things we simply would not see otherwise. The particular quality of the lens of the cross is paradox. What seems impossible is somehow possible. Two realities co-exist, even contradictory realities. Jesus Christ is crucified and suffers a humiliating and painful death on the cross, yet because of his obedient bearing of the cross Jesus Christ is resurrected, exalted, victorious, and brings salvation to humanity. Two paradoxical realities are attached to the cross, even though in human understanding two simultaneously opposing yet true realities simply defeats logic.

Paul grasped this fundamental paradoxical quality of the cross as an essential component of the Christian life: "We are treated as deceivers and

1. Sanderson, *Alcatraz*.

yet are truthful; as unrecognized and yet acknowledged; as dying and behold we live; as chastised and yet not put to death; as sorrowful yet always rejoicing; as poor yet enriching many; as having nothing and yet possessing all things" (2 Cor 6:8–10). Paul realized that his new Christian communities needed to be able to see and interpret their lives through the essential lens of the cross of Jesus Christ—they needed specially-crafted eyeglasses to see the truth of things. However, Paul did not arrive at this profound insight immediately. First he had to work through a seriously disturbing issue. He had to work through the fact that he had missed recognizing the crucified Jesus Christ as the Jewish messiah until divine light intervened and literally changed his sight. He had to work through the deeply troubling and paradoxical truth that God had been crucified.

To understand how central the paradox of the cross truly was to the identity and thought of Paul the convert, we must at least briefly consider what the cross must have signified to a first-century Pharisee such as Paul. Not only did Jews abhor the Roman practice of crucifixion because it was used to subjugate Judea and represented the despicable punishment of slaves and criminals, they viewed it with special contempt because according to Jewish law as expressed in Deut 21:23, those hanged on a tree were cursed by God. Therefore, from a Jewish perspective, "[a] crucified man was a societal reject; but a crucified god was a contradiction in terms."[2] That Paul the Pharisee likely considered this to be the case, and moreover blasphemy, is suggested by his pre-conversion efforts to persecute the Church[3] and by his citation of Deut 21:23 in Gal 3:13, "Christ ransomed us from the curse of the law by becoming a curse for us, for it is written, 'Cursed be everyone who hangs on a tree.'" His post-conversion perception of the crucifixion was therefore deeply informed by a sensibility of God acting outside the parameters of human expectation and understanding in a way only graspable through the medium of paradox.

From a first-century Jewish perspective, Jesus Christ did not fit the preconceived form of the Jewish messiah, nor did his earthly life reflect the expected trajectory of the Jewish messiah. He was, in fact, in humble and humiliated form; his life a humble and crucified path. Paul discovered within this very contradiction two important aspects of the paradox of the cross. First, the humility of the cross at least initially concealed its glory, and therefore its nature was not only paradoxical, but also *hidden* in and

2. Green, "The Folly of the Cross," 66.

3. See, e.g., Acts 8:1, 3; 9:1–2.

through the paradox. Second, the ostensible emptiness and futility of the crucifixion was powerfully countered by the supreme *effectiveness* of divine action. What I mean by this is simply that God is effective in accomplishing his will, even in or through the most unlikely or dire circumstances.[4] God chooses over and over again throughout salvation history to show his unbounded power to act even through the most limited or humble circumstances and people. We find the ultimate example of God's unfettered effectiveness in the paradox of the cross: humiliation, pain and death become glory, resurrection, and the salvation of humanity. For Paul, the paradox of the cross could not be separated from these two qualities of hiddenness and divine effectiveness.

Once Paul had seized on the paradox of the cross, he realized it held the key to interpretation. It provided the lens through which he and all Christians should examine experience. In choosing "Christ crucified"[5] as the central force and message of his public ministry, Paul places the impossible possible at the center of his theology and preaching. He wanted his young communities to absorb the paradox inherent in the cross and apply it to more than simply an understanding of the crucifixion. He wanted them, and us, to understand the paradox of the cross as a wellspring for Christian life. Paul experienced this paradoxical contrast not only in the Christ event, but in his own person, in his life, in circumstances impacting the new communities, in the communities themselves, and in the person and lives of each individual follower of Christ.

The paradigm-shattering paradox of the cross finds expression through myriad paradoxical contrasts throughout Paul's letters. Almost as if examining the pure light of the crucifixion as shot through a prism, Paul speaks of this central paradox in a spectrum of insights: life in death (1 Cor 15:36, 43; 2 Cor 4:9–11, 5:9, 7:3; Phil 1:21); power in weakness (1 Cor 1:26–28, 15:43; 2 Cor 12:9–10; Phil 2:6–11); gain in loss (Phil 3:7–8); renewal in wasting away (2 Cor 4:16); salvation in destruction (Phil 1:28); wisdom in what others consider foolishness (1 Cor 1:18–25, 2:14; 3:18–19); victory in apparent defeat (1 Cor 15:54–57); joy in suffering (Phil 2:17; cf. 2 Cor 6:10, 7:4). He clearly demarks those who perceive, and can live out of, the paradox as those who live by the spirit (Rom 8:4–6; 1 Cor 2:12; Gal

---

4. For a development of the scriptural underpinning of divine effectiveness which arises from Pauline *metalepsis*, or intertextual echo, of Isa 55:10–13 in Phil 2:6–11, see Hogan, *Pauline Theology*, 50–88.

5. 1 Cor 1:23; see also 1 Cor 2:2.

5:16–18, 22–25), or are citizens of heaven (Phil 3:3, 20); the contrast is to those who are still in the flesh (Rom 8:6, 7–8; Gal 5:17–21), the worldly (1 Cor 2:12), "the enemies of the cross of Christ" (Phil 3:18) whose "minds are occupied with earthly things" (Phil 3:19), those who cannot perceive (1 Cor 2:14). Paul frames this perceptual difference in terms of belonging and citizenship—the heavenly, who live in the spirit, versus the earthly, who live still in the flesh.

Notice that each one of these paradoxical contrasts is instructional. They teach us to perceive something full of life, victory, and goodness which lies *hidden* under the appearance of something deathly, empty, or dark. They also teach us to perceive that even in situations which appear futile or defeating, God is ultimately *effective* to accomplish his fruitful will and victory. Each paradox utilized by Paul contains an antithetical pair, one representing the earthly perception of futility, and one representing the heavenly perception of effectiveness. Thus what appears to be loss is actually gain in the kingdom of heaven; what appears to be death is in fact life in the kingdom of heaven; what appears foolishness is wisdom; what appears to be our destruction is our salvation; what appears weak has strength; what appears cause for sorrow is actually cause for joy.

Thus we can see that Paul uses paradox throughout his letters to describe the difference between the earthly perspective and the corresponding heavenly perspective, in which one can perceive the true and effective state of things even when they are hidden. The one who grasps and can apply this paradox to her life and her person holds the key to accurately perceiving the two realities and placing greater value on the heavenly perspective. Remember our little bird from the last chapter? An ordinary mystic has a sense of both earthly and heavenly realities, and this dual perspective can be understood as the lens of the cross. Why did Francis of Assisi renounce his possessions and live a life of poverty? Why did Mother Teresa go to Calcutta and minister to the impoverished and dying? Why did Maximilian Kolbe take the place of a man chosen for the gas chamber? They all perceived the heavenly reality and chose it over earthly concerns.

Paul realized that his most urgent pastoral task was teaching his young communities to live out of this paradox, to perceive the existence of the heavenly reality in contrast to the often stark and dire earthly circumstances of first-century Christian life. Paul's concern was not so much about survival, or even encouragement, but about providing new Christians with the key to their very being. True reflection of Christ, and transformation in and through Christ, depended upon this shift in perception.

Paul did not simply teach this in a vacuum. He supported his exhortations repeatedly by offering concrete and personal illustrations. As one example among several, the Letter to the Philippians demonstrates Paul's consistent and methodical encouragement to this shift in perspective. Paul begins his letter with a prayer for the Philippians which sets the tone for the entire letter:

> And this is my prayer: that your love may increase ever more and more in knowledge and every kind of perception, to discern what is of value, so that you may be pure and blameless for the day of Christ, filled with the fruit of righteousness that comes through Jesus Christ for the glory and praise of God.[6]

Perception and discernment of true value—seeing true reality—is the core endeavor of the Christian. Paul makes it clear that true reality may be hidden under contrary worldly appearances or worldly wisdom by immediately offering three examples. First, he explains that, paradoxically, the crushing event of his imprisonment "has turned out rather to advance the gospel" (Phil 1:12) since it has become well known, and has offered encouragement to others who proclaim the gospel (1:13–14). Second, even though the gospel is proclaimed by those who "preach Christ from envy and rivalry" (1:15), it has not a negative but a positive impact—Christ is proclaimed (1:18). Third, Paul himself, whether his imprisonment ends in life or in death, will magnify Christ (1:20). The message is clear in all three examples—victory comes out of apparent defeat, gain comes out of apparent loss, life comes out of apparent death. Moreover, this perception of the true reality of things, and the real and present victory gained for and through Christ, is cause for joy (1:18).

Before I tell you more about Paul and his further development of this stunning and paradoxical understanding, let me give you an example from my own life that helped me to see that I may not perceive the truth of things even when I think I do. In February of 1994 my father was diagnosed with an unusual form of cancer, carcinoid cancer. The cancer developed in his intestines and metastasized to his liver. When he was diagnosed, my dad had a grapefruit-sized tumor in his intestines, and a tennis ball-sized tumor in his liver in addition to smaller tumors. Obviously, his cancer was

---

6. Phil 1:9–11 (compare Rom 12:2; 16:19).

in an advanced state. He was able to have surgery to remove the cancerous part of his intestines, but all the cancerous tumors could not be removed surgically from his liver. At that time a new way medicine was addressing this problem in cancer patients was by giving transplants. If an organ was cancerous but inoperable, the theory went, why not replace the organ with a transplant? So my father went on the transplant list in 1995. We waited with bated breath for months and the call finally came. He went into surgery, but in the process of liberating his liver for the transplant, the surgeons discovered inoperable cancer outside of the liver. So they did not do the transplant. This news was devastating to my father when he awoke from the unsuccessful surgery, and devastating to me. To us it meant one thing—certain and near death.

However, as the months and years unfolded following this "no-transplant transplant," as my dad liked to refer to it, a strange thing happened. Several cancer patients around my father who had been transplanted successfully with a new liver begin to die. The immunosuppression drugs one had to take following a transplant compromised the immune system's ability to fight off recurrences of cancer. So if the cancer recurred, as it did in some of these patients, death came swiftly. As it happened, using other forms of cancer therapy, my father lived for another six years after the no-transplant transplant—he died on October 11, 2001, seven years and seven and a half months after his diagnosis. As we slowly learned, what we and the medical experts thought meant impending death for my dad actually meant significantly more life. The no-transplant transplant was, paradoxically, life under the appearance of death.

Of course, I could not know about this paradoxical outcome in advance of it transpiring, and I could also be missing paradox in events happening all around me today. However, I gained a new openness through this experience, a new appreciation that God may be operating in a way mysterious to my intellectual understanding. I gained a new awareness of the possibility of paradox, and of the reality of God's ways being far above my ways, and God's thoughts being far above my thoughts. I began to see evidence of the paradox of the cross operating in my daily life, that what seems like loss and dying might actually be gain and life. Perhaps most importantly, I could trace the presence of God with us throughout this event, and God's unmistakable effectiveness to accomplish his good even in or through dark situations. Once you have the sure grasp that God is present with you always, and working all things for good in his own ways, suddenly the darkness is pierced by light.

So when Paul tells us that victory may come from defeat, gain from loss, and life from death, and gives us examples from his own life, he is urging us that the theology of the paradox of the cross is real, concrete, and urgently important to understand as Christians. He wanted young Christian communities to live out of the hope and joy of the promise of the resurrection, and *not to stop in defeat at the first sign of crucifixion*. He wanted them, and us, to see signs of loss, defeat, pain, and even death as more than they appeared to be, because that is the message of the cross of Jesus—"If, then, we have died with Christ, we believe that we shall also live with him" (Rom 6:8). This paradox of the cross is the key to interpreting our life experience as Christians.

Paul takes this a step further in his Letter to the Philippians. Not only is detection of the paradoxical true reality of paramount interpretative concern, it is essential also to the *identity* of followers of Christ, and as such the true reality of things must be sought out and embraced by the Philippians. Therefore, their struggles (1:27–28), suffering (1:29), and community interaction (2:1–4) must be viewed from the perspective of uncovered paradox, through the mind and lens of Christ: "Have among yourselves the same attitude that is also yours in Christ Jesus" (2:5). He follows this exhortation with the splendid Christ Hymn (2:6–11) which probes the paradox of the crucifixion—Christ, "though he was in the form of God" (2:6), empties himself (2:7), humbles himself, and is crucified (2:8); as a result, "God greatly exalted him" (2:9), which has a transformative impact upon humanity (2:10–11). What by earthly standards would appear to be death, destruction, humiliation, and defeat is radically reversed in the heavenly— Christ is exalted by God, given "the name that is above every name" (2:9), and all are subject to him and confess him as Lord (2:10–11), a most glorious and effective victory. Paul points to and proclaims this central paradox as the new and defining paradigm.[7]

---

7. "When he was put to death on the cross he seemed to have labored in vain. But by raising him from the dead God has saved him, vindicated him, and is now making him the means of salvation to non-Jews as well as to Israel." Hanson, *Paradox of the Cross*, 56. Moreover, this efficacy extends to Christians: "[Paul] now emphasizes by means of this citation [Isa 49:8 in 2 Cor 6:2] that Christ's vindication also belongs to Christians. . . . We may understand that Paul is using this Isaiah citation in order to assure the Corinthians that as they share in the sufferings of Christ they also share in his vindication." Ibid. Hanson focuses upon efficacy even in apparent vanity as expressed in Isa 49:4 as the key meaning of this Isaiah reference by Paul in 2 Cor 6:2: "But I said, 'I have labored in vain,/

Moreover, in the same way that Paul exhorts the Philippians to the attitude of Christ and perspective governed by heavenly rather than earthly concerns, Paul also exhibits that perspective himself. Paul offers himself as an example of self-sacrificing service (2:17), considering all loss for the gain of Christ (3:7–9), and single-minded focus upon the attainment of Christ (3:12–14). His fundamentally-altered perspective is now defined by Christ alone, therefore he lives the paradox: sacrifice and suffering are undertaken with joy; the "loss of all things" is considered desirable because Christ is gained; even memory and previous self, "what lies behind," is forgotten in favor of the goal of Christ. Paul sees, embraces, and exemplifies the paradigm shift which characterizes the new creation of Christ.

Just as Paul spoke to the Philippians, Paul also speaks to us today in our own personal lives and situations. Paul wants us also to perceive the paradoxical pattern of the crucified Lord, repeated in Paul, and in the Philippians, and apply it to our own hearts, minds, thoughts, and actions. Can we take the paradox of the cross as a lens through which to interpret events and people in our own lives? Sometimes when we face a challenge or a loss or a devastating event, it is too hard to allow for the presence of such a paradox. Sometimes we may feel that we will never catch a glimpse of it. But sometimes we are given direct experience of it. When we do experience the paradox of the cross in our own lives, whether in a small event or in a major one, we need to hold onto it as a precious gift. God has given us invaluable experiential insight into the Christian paradox.

The lives of the saints provide us with countless examples of this paradoxical quality, which, remember, contains elements of hiddenness and divine effectiveness. John of the Cross was imprisoned and brutally beaten, yet somehow in that prison composed one of the most beautiful theological poems ever written, which later gave rise to his extraordinary theology of the *Dark Night of the Soul*; ultimately John was proclaimed a saint and a Doctor of the Church. Teresa of Avila says that she suffered great misery at the hands of confessors who did not understand her, yet through this trial she grew to trust in her relationship with God rather than rely on the faulty human intellect of her priestly advisors. If she had not developed that sense of trust in her own sense of God and God's relationship with her, we might never have had her *Interior Castle* and other great works; she also was named a saint and Doctor of the Church. Thérèse of Lisieux

---

I have spent my strength for nothing and vanity;/ but surely my right is with the Lord,/ and my recompense with my God.'" Isa 49:4; Hanson, *Paradox of the Cross*, 55.

felt trapped and confined by her circumstances of being a youthful and enclosed nun rather than an apostle, priest or someone who could extraordinarily proclaim the gospel. Yet it was this very limitation that gave her the insight that she could express extraordinary love in each ordinary moment. Through this "little way" she became a saint and a Doctor of the Church.

These examples might seem extreme; after all, these three became saints and Doctors of the Church. But look at the circumstances in which they found themselves: a violent imprisonment; an ordeal of self-doubt and questioning coupled with public misunderstanding and slander; and an experience of obscurity and smallness. Those events have, and indeed do, happen to more than a few of us. Imagine if we, like the saints, could attach a relentless and enduring love of Jesus Christ and the paradox of his cross to our own challenging experience?

In the case of a whole life lived, hindsight is twenty-twenty; one can perceive the paradox lived out, the hiddenness revealed, the ultimate triumph of divine effectiveness. But what about those of us in the midst of living, we whose lives are a story still unfolding? How do we even begin to perceive the paradox? Perhaps it helps to remember that just as Paul, John, Teresa, and Thérèse did, we live in our present circumstances. We live subject to time and space and events and people. We have a particular set of circumstances each day. Perhaps the best way to begin our effort to perceive Paul's paradox of the cross, to perceive both the earthly and heavenly realities, is to open ourselves to the idea that there could be a different and unexpected interpretation of events.

A friend of mine who is a sister of the Congregation of the Sisters of the Holy Faith provides a wonderful contemporary example of this shift in perspective. Sr. Mary experienced a horrible fall down a flight of stairs and was seriously injured. She spent several painful months in first a hospital and then a convalescent center. Her recovery was markedly slow and made particularly uncomfortable by a body brace which kept her confined to a bed most of the time. During this period of time she encountered many people who came and went in and out of her room and her life, and she found herself sharing the gospel and ministering to many of these people in unexpected ways. At last, after months and months of recovery, she was able to leave the convalescent center. She was gracious enough to attend my thesis defense, during which I presented Paul's paradox of the cross and his perception of a hidden and divine effectiveness even in a dire and painful situation. Directly afterward she exclaimed to me, "I know why I was in the hospital all that time! I was Paul in prison. That was exactly where I needed to be to proclaim the gospel." She was able to look past the earthly perspective of the intense suffering and loss of time and mobility, and perceive the event in light of the heavenly perspective of the deeply effective way she had touched lives through her impromptu ministry while in the hospital.

Sr. Mary's experience also illustrates the definite and sometimes harsh divide and discrepancy between earthly and heavenly perspectives. The earthly experience of intense suffering does not seem to mesh with or even touch upon the heavenly. Yet we can paradoxically experience both realities simultaneously in a given situation, just as Paul did in prison, and Sr. Mary did in the hospital.

The mystic is keenly aware of this discrepancy between the two realities. The mystical experience, whether extraordinary or ordinary, connects the soul deeply with God. The touch of God transports and transforms—yet the mystic remains earthbound in the end, awkwardly both a heavenly citizen and earthly inhabitant. The discrepancy between being simultaneously a citizen of heaven and a resident of earth inevitably results in trial—earthly existence demands a response to that discrepancy. The mystic's glimpses of something beyond the natural flood the soul with keen awareness of the truth of heavenly reality, yet the natural engulfs it outwardly, with all the standards, expectations, requirements, and suffering of natural reality. Even in the complete embrace of the heavenly reality, the earthly trial is nevertheless quite real, rooted firmly and painfully in our lives and personhood. The challenge that constantly presents itself is the break, the divide between the two realities pressing upon the followers of Jesus, at both the individual and community levels.

Crucially (and paradoxically), both realities may be said to be true. "The phrase 'dying and behold we live' is uttered from the standpoint of the believer: he knows of the hidden life. But the outward man really is in a state of dying."[8] As another example, two paradoxical realities may exist in terms of weakness and power. Paul experienced real and present weakness such as the "thorn in the flesh" (2 Cor 12:7), yet also experienced power in weakness, saying "when I am weak, then I am strong" (2 Cor 12:10). The important thing to grasp here is that, "[i]t is not that Paul was once weak but now made strong; *in the midst* of Paul's 'weakness' God's power is revealed."[9] Two simultaneous and paradoxical realities pervaded Paul's ex-

8. Ibid., 66 (quoting 2 Cor 6:9).

9. Cousar, *Theology of the Cross*, 167.

perience. Could we say the same of ourselves? If we may begin to perceive it, in the midst of things humiliated, weak, deathly, dark and painful, we may be also real and powerful conduits and revealers of God and his divine effectiveness.

Existence in the natural reality while embracing the perspective of the supernatural reality becomes a reflection in the world of this break or chasm between heavenly and earthly. As pointing to something beyond the world, it can hardly be expressed in terms of the world, and as such appears hidden or humiliated. The choice for the soul then is one of perspective—shall it see this present trial as a vain exercise, one dividing it further from everything it knows? Or shall it see it as effective, mysteriously uniting it ever closer to the author of the heavenly? For Paul the answer is straightforward: "this momentary light affliction is *producing for us* an eternal weight of glory beyond all comparison, as we look not to what is seen but to what is unseen; for what is seen is transitory, but what is unseen is eternal" (2 Cor 4:17–18, emphasis added). Paul sees the trial from the heavenly perspective—enduring the earthly trial is effective to render something glorious in the heavenly.

Paul urges us to perceive the endurance of the earthly trial with eyes on the heavenly upward calling in Christ Jesus as the crucial race or fight of our lives. He encourages us not to be distracted by the world or convinced by the world's wisdom that the effort and endurance required by the race and the fight is all for nothing. In fact, the lens of the cross reveals the opposite to us. Our run, our fight, is serious and urgent.

> Do you not know that the runners in the stadium all run in the race, but only one wins the prize? Run so as to win. Every athlete exercises discipline in every way. They do it to win a perishable crown, but we an imperishable one. Thus I do not run aimlessly; I do not fight as if I were shadowboxing.[10]

The message is clear: fight with purpose to endure the earthly trial without taking your eyes off the heavenly prize. Seen through the lens of the cross, the effort and suffering required is of little import when viewed in the light of what is achieved from the heavenly perspective.

Paul's analogy remains apt today. A contemporary boxer trains for hours a day to endure physical pain so that during the fight he can persevere through pain. The boxer learns to interpret that pain as something

---

10. 1 Cor 9:24–26.

that must be endured for the sake of winning the fight. The pain thresh-
old is increased through conditioning, training, and through the mental
grasp of what is gained through the endurance of the pain.[11] Paul clearly
understood that the trial for the Christian was the gap between the earthly
trial and the heavenly prize. If the Christian could be disciplined enough
to interpret what she had to endure for the sake of Christ as simply part of
the necessary and crucial fight for her upward calling in Christ Jesus, then
this shift in perspective would be a powerful weapon in the fight. Like a
boxer who keeps on fighting regardless of pain indicates his competitive
and single-minded focus on a perishable prize, the Christian who keeps on
fighting the "good fight" (1 Tim 1:18) of faith despite earthly appearances
reveals not only her single-hearted love of God and focus on the imperish-
able heavenly prize, but also the hidden and effective kingdom of God.

Wait a minute, you might be saying. I am definitely not a professional
boxer or an elite runner. The idea of that kind of discipline and endurance
physically or even spiritually seems alien and beyond my capacity. How
could Paul have meant this for someone like me?

Paul did mean it for you. He meant it for each of us, even we who
know we are the little birds of Thérèse's imagination. The little bird is precisely the warrior of Paul's urging, the one who might not believe in her
capacity to arrive at the victory. The little bird has the heart and mind to
desire the victory and yet at least ostensibly lacks the wherewithal in her
person, life circumstances or other resources to achieve the victory. Yet
hidden in the heart and the mind of the little bird is the potential for great
and effective victory. The little bird only has to begin by seeing herself and
her life through the paradox of the cross—that hidden even in smallness,
darkness, and frailty is great and effective potential to proclaim God in and
through her very being and life.

Once while driving to pick up my children from school, I saw a very
little songbird flying fast and close to a much larger bird, perhaps a crow.
The crow shot ahead, dodging and dancing this way and that, and the songbird kept chasing its tail fiercely, matching it movement for movement. The
pair shot by me and were gone in an instant, but the image of the little bird
pressing the much larger crow so furiously stayed with me. I learned later
that this behavior of smaller birds chasing and driving off much larger birds
stems from a desire in the bird to protect its young. The seemingly over-
matched little bird lets the singled-minded fire of protecting its nest drive

11. I am indebted to David Rivello for sharing his boxing expertise.

it beyond fear to risk a David and Goliath confrontation. Moreover, this behavior in smaller birds individually or collectively is highly successful in driving away larger predator birds.

In a similar way that God equipped David with small stones and a slingshot to bring down Goliath, God equips the little bird with the lens of the cross to arrive at her victory. With a faithful single-minded focus on the heavenly, the little bird overcomes, lets God's glory shine through, slays giants with precisely who she is and what she has, even and especially using ordinary things like five smooth stones from the river and determination. The little bird is paradoxically a mighty warrior precisely because, according to Paul, "power is made perfect in weakness" (2 Cor 12:9).

For Paul, because the Christian trial lies in the discrepancy between the earthly and heavenly realities, so does the battlefield. The boxing ring and the track stadium of his analogy are located in everyday life events. Paul's exhortation to us is about our commitment to show up for this fight. Can we persevere through trial, small or large? Can we be steadfast in our perception of God's hidden and effective action in and through circumstances which may appear futile or empty? That is the battle of the Christian, even for one who is a little bird. The wherewithal to do battle by earthly standards is not relevant. As Paul says, "although we are in the flesh, we do not battle according to the flesh, for the weapons of our battle are not of flesh but are enormously powerful, capable of destroying fortresses" (2 Cor 10:3–4). Paul knew well that the most valiant warriors were those whose hearts love God and whose minds grasp and assimilate the paradox of the cross, and thus "take every thought captive" (2 Cor 10:5) in order to reshape it according to the pattern of Jesus Christ.

While the cross of Jesus Christ may at first glance seem as impenetrable and indecipherable as Alcatraz's mysterious bag of sand, when we begin to realize that the cross holds the key to understanding the true state of things, it is worth the all-out battle to make it our own, in thought and in action. Paul recognized the defining quality of the lens of the cross as paradox, and consequently employed paradox for the purpose of describing Christian experience, which is marked by simultaneous yet contrasting earthly and heavenly realities. Similar to Alcatraz, the Christian needs to put on her paradox of the cross eyeglasses to accurately perceive and attach value to the true state of things. The paradoxes used by Paul in his writings, such as life in death, wisdom in foolishness, gain in loss, and so on, each reflect two qualities Paul found inherent in the paradox of the cross:

hiddenness and divine effectiveness. A fruitful and life-giving heavenly reality exists hidden under an earthly reality's contrasting appearance of futility and emptiness. Moreover, the heavenly reality contains divine effectiveness—that is, God is effective to accomplish fruitfulness and his divine purpose even in and through dark or dire circumstances. Encouragement of his fledgling communities, and us, to this shift in perspective from the earthly to the heavenly, was a key and urgent task for Paul, for he viewed this paradigm shift as essential to accurate discernment of what is of true value. However, as Paul found in his communities and in his own life, the discrepancy in daily life between these two realities inevitably gives rise to trial. Paul urges all of us, even those of us who consider ourselves little birds who are small and without much capacity, to persevere with resolve and keep our eyes fixed on the heavenly reality even as we run our course and fight our way through the earthly reality. Paul captures the sense of divine effectiveness even in paradoxical and hidden circumstances in his impassioned plea for his communities, and us, to "be firm, steadfast, always fully devoted to the work of the Lord, knowing that in the Lord your labor is not in vain" (1 Cor 15:58). Despite all appearances, we perceive that the victory is already in hand.

Chapter 3

A Map Left Behind

The Living Pattern of the Christ Hymn

DESPITE THE BEST EFFORTS of modern linguists, ancient Egyptian hieroglyphics remained untranslatable until a marvelous key to understanding them was discovered in 1799. The Rosetta Stone provided new and stunning clarity to translation of the unintelligible language. Because the hieroglyphics were one of three scripts inscribed on an Egyptian stele with the identical text of a 196 BC decree by Ptolemy V, linguists could use the other two known languages to crack the code of the hieroglyphics. What initially appeared to be just another stone repurposed as building material ended up having great importance as the key to uncovering the meaning of a previously incomprehensible mystery.

What if such a key existed that could help us understand the person and mystery of Jesus Christ? What if there were some touchtone text which could point us in the correct direction, give us the shape and the pattern of not only Christ, but also who we are called to be in Christ? What if someone who knew Christ wanted to provide the key to our understanding of him, a map of the contours and pathways of our upward calling in Christ Jesus?

Such a text does exist. Our touchstone is found in Paul's Letter to the Philippians, in verses 2:6–11, and is known as the Christ Hymn. "Have among yourselves the same attitude (or mind) that is also yours in Christ Jesus," Paul announces in Philippians verse 2:5, indicating that what he is about to say reveals something important about not only Jesus Christ, but also his followers. As if inspired to express the living form of Jesus Christ in image and sound and pattern, Paul traces his divine outline:

6   Who, though he was in the form of God,
        did not regard equality with God
            something to be grasped.

7   Rather, he emptied himself,
        taking the form of a slave,
        coming in human likeness;
        and found human in appearance,

8   he humbled himself,
        becoming obedient to death,
            even death on a cross.

9   Because of this, God greatly exalted him
        and bestowed on him the name
        that is above every name,

10   that at the name of Jesus
        every knee should bend,
        of those in heaven and on earth and
            under the earth,

11   and every tongue confess that
        Jesus Christ is Lord,
        to the glory of God the Father.

Phil 2:6–11.

The ancient hieroglyphics on the Rosetta Stone may have seemed dense and incomprehensible at first glance, but they yielded their secret language after some patient detection of pattern. The Christ Hymn also contains a detectable landscape of movement and pattern which reveals much about not only Jesus Christ, but all Christians.

Viewed this way, perhaps the first thing we notice about this language is the plummeting and rising motion of the text. Can you detect a "V-shape" here, a pattern of descending and ascending by the subject of the hymn, Jesus Christ? He begins at the highest point—"the form of God" (2:6). He "emptied himself" (2:7), which marks the beginning of his descent. Through voluntary self-abasement he descends even further, "taking the form of a slave" (2:7). He reaches the nadir, which is also the midpoint of the hymn, with his obedience to the point of death, "even death on a cross" (2:8). Then Christ begins from the lowest point to ascend because God exalts him (2:9). At his name alone "every knee shall bend" (2:10), and he reaches the highest point once again as he is restored to his rightful position of "Lord, to the glory of God the Father" (2:11). One scholar, Bruce Fisk, gives us this visual representation of the "V-shape" of the Christ Hymn:

6	Though he was in the form of God,
	he did not regard equality with God as something to be exploited,
7	but emptied himself,
	taking the form of a slave,
	being born in human likeness.
	And being found in human form,
8	he humbled himself
	and became obedient to the point of death—
	even death on a cross.
9	Therefore God also highly exalted him
	and gave him the name that is above every name,
10	so at the name of Jesus every knee should bend,
	in heaven and on earth and under the earth,
11	and every tongue should confess that Jesus Christ is Lord,
	to the glory of God the Father.

Fisk, "The Odyssey of Christ," 49.

We can detect a clear pattern of descending and ascending not only in the text, but in the person of Jesus Christ.

Can you also perceive something hidden and yet effective about this pattern? Jesus Christ "emptied himself," took "the form of a slave," and not only "humbled himself," but died a humiliating "death on a cross." This descent into apparent oblivion appears humble, humiliated, empty and deathly. Yet look at the ascending side of our "V-shape," which functions to reveal the otherwise hidden yet effective heavenly reality of the actions of Jesus Christ: he is "exalted" by God, and given "the name that is above every name," which also enables humans to worship him and confess him in their own actions and words. The actions of Jesus Christ were supremely effective not only in his own restoration and exaltation, but significantly, were effective to cause a crucially important change in humankind—they are empowered to confess and express Jesus Christ in and though their actions and their words, in and through their very lives. Thus we may detect the wellspring of the qualities of hiddenness and divine effectiveness perceived so insightfully by Paul: they are present in the person and story of Jesus Christ, and consequently of his followers.

This movement in the life and person of Jesus is reinforced and echoed in other scripture. For example, in the Gospel of John, Jesus says, "I came from the Father and have come into the world. Now I am leaving the world and going back to the Father" (John 16:28). Elsewhere in John we have Jesus describing the effect of his death: "And when I am lifted up from the earth, I will draw everyone to myself" (John 12:32). Imagine, then, not simply a trajectory of Jesus descending and then Jesus ascending; but rather Jesus descending, being with us here on earth, and then Jesus ascending and drawing us up after him. Envision a magnet swooping down to metal filings and then rising again, all the while magnetically attracting and drawing up the filings, which have become a chain of mini-magnets themselves. Jesus comes not just to come and go, but for the express purpose of lifting and drawing us up after him, as we in turn reflect and live out his shape and pattern.

In fact, the motion of the Christ Hymn can be broken down into three parts, or three moments in the relationship between God and us. First, Jesus Christ *empties* himself, for the loving purpose of coming to us. Second, Jesus Christ is profoundly *with us*, in the form of a human being who lived, breathed, loved, taught, shared, and died among us. Third, Jesus Christ is exalted by God and humans are enabled to confess and express Jesus Christ in their words and actions, in a saving and *transforming unity* which draws humans up after him.

Each of these moments is expressive of the loving relationship between God and us: self-emptying in the first moment, or *kenosis*; Christ-with-us in the second moment, or *enosis*; and transformative divine unity in the third moment, or *theosis*. So if we could visualize such a pattern in the Christ Hymn, it might look like this:

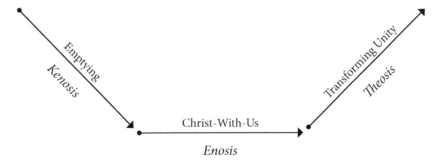

Consider these three words *kenosis*, *enosis*, and *theosis* as shorthand for these three kinds of moments we share with God: emptying or suffering moments; experience of God-with-us in creation and people; and moments of experience of unity with the divine.[1] Let's take a closer look at each of these three moments of divine-human relationship.

Kenosis, both the word itself and the theology which has grown up around it, has as its source the Christ Hymn, and specifically Phil 2:7, "he emptied himself."[2] The chief idea underlying *kenosis* is radical emptying of self as a key characteristic of Jesus Christ, and as such a key characteristic also of his disciples, and one key aspect of their spiritual experience. The profundity of the *kenosis* of Christ cannot be overemphasized: "Not only did Christ take the form of a lowly slave but he appeared as the lowliest and most despised of persons by being put to death on a Cross."[3] This extremity reveals a radical love which embraces and unifies itself with "the 'no-things' of this world,"[4] and moreover calls for a corresponding response. *Kenosis* is associated with the giving over of oneself in conformity with Christ; this self-emptying involves self-sacrifice in the sense that it predicates loss, or suffering, or even death; it involves identification with the weak and lowly. *Kenosis* breaks down the self in favor of Christ and his concerns. In Paul's experience of Christ, *kenosis* involves some of the elements we touched upon earlier in connection with self, namely, the setting aside of former perceptions and selfhood in favor of Christ and participation in the life of Christ. Crucially, Paul sees suffering as something to be shared with Christ (Phil 3:10), and participation in the sufferings of Christ has a transformative effect—conformity to, and union with, Christ.

Enosis is a term which expresses a moment of Christ-with-us as experienced in creation and community, and I use it here as it arises from Phil 2:7–8, "coming in human likeness; and found human in appearance,

---

1. Keith Ward identifies the three moments of the divine relationship to the cosmos as *kenosis, enosis*, and *theosis*. Ward, "Cosmos and Kenosis," 152–166.

2. The term "*kenosis*" derives from the Phil 2:7 usage of the verb κενόω (to empty or to make void). A wide variety of interpretations has given rise to a theology of *kenosis*, in which Phil 2:7 was "taken as a real self-relinquishing, limiting, or emptying of divine attributes, powers, prerogatives, and/or glory by the pre-existent Logos upon the event of Incarnation." Thompson, "Nineteenth Century Kenotic Christology," 75. For the range of interpretations of Phil 2:7, see Martin, *Carmen Christi*. Thompson's treatment provides an analysis of nineteenth-century interpretations.

3. Power, *Love Without Calculation*, 7.

4. Ibid., 32.

he humbled himself, becoming obedient to death, even death on a cross." As Christ took on human likeness and appearance, and came among us, to live and to die like us, he was profoundly with us. In a fullness of union with creation undoubtedly beyond our grasp, Christ not only became man through the mystery of the Incarnation, but in humility lived out a life which encompassed and embraced our human experience in total: from joy to suffering, king to slave, riches to poverty, cherished son to tortured criminal, majesty to utter humiliation, the Godhead to the extreme nadir, the lowest point of human experience. Through the actions described in Phil 2:7–8, Christ gathered humanity into his embrace in a definitive moment of "with-us": of being and living with us here on earth, of literally breathing with us in our humanity,[5] and of walking, teaching, loving, and struggling like us, even to the point of a painful and humiliating death. The moment of *enosis*, then, is the experience of Christ-with-us, in and through creation, which includes human beings and nature, and as found in the bonds of community. Here in this moment, in the very heartbeat of human existence, divine meets human in intimate sharing and loving presence in both individual and communal contexts. Paul's writings witness abundantly to his experience of Christ-with-us, a concept most vividly illustrated in the recurring Pauline metaphor of Christian community as the body of Christ.

Theosis refers to the transformation of the person as God draws her into union with himself, through which the person is enabled to reflect the likeness or image of God,[6] and I employ it here as arising from Phil

---

5. In choosing to take human form, Jesus Christ embraced the weakness and fragility of humanity, and joined with us in a deeply participatory σύμπνοια, "breathing together;" an action taken up and continued by the Holy Spirit at Pentecost (Acts 2:2–4). John 20:22 directly associates the breath of Jesus with the Holy Spirit. See Kilcourse, "Breath, Breathing," 105–106.

6. *Theosis* or *theopoiesis*, a process also sometimes called divinization or deification, has deep roots in Christian tradition. Elements of this doctrine may be found in the thought of Plato and Plotinus, and arose in connection with Christianity first in the work of Origen. As Andrew Louth explains, for Origen, "[k]nowing God is being known by God, and that means that God is united to those who know him, and gives them a share in his divinity. So, knowing God means divinization, *theopoiesis*. Knowing God is having the image of God, which we are, reformed after the likeness: the image is perfected so that we are like God. And contemplation is the means of this, for contemplation is, for Origen, a *transforming* vision." Louth, *Origins of the Christian Mystical Tradition*, 73. The origin of the doctrine of *theosis* is traditionally associated with Athanasius (c. 296–373), who wrote in *De Incarnatione*, "For he [the Word] became man that we might become divine." Athanasius, "De Incarnatione," § 54. But the doctrine also has earlier roots in the work of Irenaeus of Lyons (c. 120–202). The *Catechism of the Catholic Church* cites 2 Pet

37

2:9–11—as Jesus was exalted by God the Father to his rightful position as the Lord (2:9), humans were granted the identity-shaping purpose of confession of Jesus as Lord, through their words and actions (2:10–11). Thus confession of the person of Jesus Christ is indelibly and inextricably linked to human identity, words, and action. True confession of Jesus Christ is precisely living in and through Jesus Christ. *Theosis*, then, is that divine transformative action through which humans are granted the ever-increasing ability to confess and express Jesus Christ in and through their very being—they become like Christ (cf. Phil 3:21; 2 Cor 3:18), and as such, divinized instruments of God. Paul references his growing conformity to Jesus Christ throughout the text of Philippians (e.g., 3:7–11), and explicitly acknowledges his "possession" by Jesus Christ as the perfecting source of this transformation (Phil 3:12).[7] Paul recognizes and desires this transformative unity with Christ: he wishes to "gain Christ and be found in him" (Phil 3:8–9), he wishes to magnify Christ "whether by life or by death" (1:20), he strains forward to take reciprocal possession of Christ (Phil 3:13); in fact, Paul's sole pursuit is toward "the goal, the prize of God's upward calling, in Christ Jesus" (Phil 3:14). As we examine *theosis* in more detail, we will see that Paul's continual experience of this transformative and divinizing union with Christ results not simply in his own transformation, but also in the transformation of others.

The Christ Hymn reveals this pattern to us, the pattern of Christ, the pattern of our relationship with the divine, and consequently our own pattern, expressed in all the moments of our lives. When we begin to know this pattern, we begin to perceive it all around us, in others, in our experience, and in our very selves. Before we examine the particular ways this pattern functions, let's consider how it might look in its broadest terms in the context of a real life today.

1:4, 2 Cor 5:17–18, Irenaeus, Athanasius, and Thomas Aquinas in its statement of the doctrine of *theosis* in catechetical instructions nos. 460, 1988, and 1999. *Catechism of the Catholic Church*, 116, 481, 484.

7. Bernard McGinn notes that although Paul "does not make use of the language of divinization" in the sense that he does not employ what later became the classic formula associated with *theosis* in Patristic thought, "his insistence on our shared sonship with Christ and the inhabiting of the spirit was to be used by later mystics to support belief that the Christian life implied a form of divinization. This divinization was conceived of as a spiritual union with God in Christ." McGinn, *Foundations of Mysticism*, 74. Michael J. Gorman finds *theosis* in Paul's letters, particularly as expressed in kenotic cruciformity. Gorman, *Inhabiting the Cruciform God*, 37.

My warmhearted, sensible, and strong friend Carolyn is battling fourth stage pancreatic cancer.[8] She has been through it all—surgeries, tests, chemotherapy, pain, lots of pain, weeks in the hospital, sleeplessness, worry for her eleven-year-old daughter, fear of what is happening to her. She is in the pit. Being a resourceful person, Carolyn identified a particular need she had in this situation and acted on it. She asked a small group of her friends to pray as a group for her, and asked me to organize the group for her. In and through this experience, I have observed moments of *kenosis, enosis,* and *theosis* which I share with you here to give you a real-life example of how these moments might play out in an individual's experience.

Kenosis is not hard to find in Carolyn's situation. She is suffering terribly in body and mind. She is in pain almost constantly. She has been "emptied" of her former life as a healthy person. She faces the increasing loss of energy and mobility. She faces the alteration of interaction with her husband and her daughter as she becomes progressively more ill. She faces the unknown. She faces fear. She faces death. She faces the loneliness of these dark and isolating circumstances. Yet even in all this, she experiences God. The way she explains it, she feels that no person can really be with her in her horrific experience. Yet when reminded that God is with her, she experiences God as truly with her in a way no one else could be, even in her suffering and darkness.

Enosis for Carolyn is found in the love and support of the people around her—her family, her friends, her caregivers, and her community; and also in the creation around her—her dog Valentine, her garden full of flowers and plants, her trees, her short walks full of the scent of jasmine or the buzz of hummingbirds. The divine is with her in all of this. As a particular example, God is with Carolyn through the friends and family in her prayer group. When we meet with her to pray as a group, she feels the presence of God. When I visit her and pray with her, somehow God makes his presence and comfort known to her through her very human friend; she writes to me, "God provides great comfort. For me you are his voice and his presence." When Carolyn was facing her most recent surgery, she posted a note to her friends and family: "Thank you for all your prayers. I have a picture in my mind of all of you surrounding me, holding hands as you stand in a circle around me, so that I am completely surrounded by your love, support and prayers." She experiences the divine in the circle of love and support of the people praying for her.

8. My friend's name has been changed.

Theosis occurring gradually within Carolyn may be glimpsed in ways she sees herself transformed by her increasing union with God. Carolyn's father passed away during her struggle with cancer, and in the aftermath she had a realization that she experienced his death differently than did her sisters. She was able to be peaceful, thankful for the long and giving life of her father, and accept his death as not so much a division from her, but more as a going ahead of her. She told me that a family member remarked on the way that she was handling the death differently than her sisters. It was this comment that gave Carolyn insight into her transformation. Additionally, when Carolyn began to perceive that one of her sisters was withdrawing slightly from her, Carolyn viewed the distancing behavior with compassion and peace, because she understood that her sister was experiencing pain related to not only her father's death, but also Carolyn's struggle with cancer. Carolyn shared this with me when she was in the hospital as a way of explaining how she could really feel a transformative shift happening within her. She later wrote in a post to her friends and family, "I never really understood what 'coming from love' meant. I've gone through a transformation over the past few months, with the help of others and through my own personal work. I feel, at a very deep level, that I now interact with individuals and the world in a completely different way. It is a beautiful personal change for me."

Carolyn's story is still unfolding. Your story is still unfolding also, day by day, moment by moment, just as my story is also. Maybe you recognized in Carolyn's story some essence of your own moments of suffering, moments of experiencing the presence of God in nature and people, or moments when you felt an unmistakable or increasing union with God. These moments can be massive or miniscule, powerful or fleeting, obvious or something so subtle that you do not recognize it for many years. God is profoundly present in each of the moments of all of our lives, if we can begin to sense and experience his presence. These three moments of *kenosis*, *enosis*, and *theosis* describe the shape of human-divine interaction. We are with God in each of these moments, whether or not we perceive his sometimes hidden presence. Moreover, when God touches, God transforms. If we allow ourselves to be with and be touched by God in these moments, God will accomplish his transformative work in us.

The Christian spiritual tradition contains echoes of this three-part way of experiencing God, which ultimately solidified in the concept of the purgative, illuminative, and unitive ways. The idea here is that a person goes through three stages in the spiritual life, experienced in a progressive order. In simplest terms, the first is the purgative way, or a stripping away of things which separate one from God. The second is the illuminative way, in which a person is granted awareness of the divine in creation. The third is the unitive way, in which the person experiences union with God. The thought of mystical theologians throughout the history of Christianity has touched upon variations on this three-part pattern repeatedly, discovering and rediscovering the three ways through various approaches. It is worth a quick look at the repeated emergence of this pattern.

The third-century Christian theologian Origen (ca. 184–253 AD) was probably the first to identify three discrete modes or ways of the mystical life.[9] An exegete at heart, Origen associated each one of these ways with scripture: purification (*ethike*) was associated with Proverbs; illumination (*physike*) was associated with Ecclesiastes; and union (*enoptike*) was associated with the Song of Songs.[10] Fourth-century Christian theologian Gregory of Nyssa (ca. 335–395 AD) understood the three ways as rooted in Moses' entry into the cloud in Exodus 20:21.[11] "[Gregory of Nyssa] speaks of the soul's progressive entry into light, cloud, and darkness: *phos*, *nephele*, and *gnophos*. This is the guiding metaphor for Gregory's understanding of the three ways. . . . The progress is a progress from light to deeper and deeper darkness."[12]

Evagrius Ponticus (345–399 AD) similarly identified three ways of the soul: *praktike*, during which the soul acquires the virtues, *physike*, during which the soul sees created reality in God, and *theologia*, or contemplation and knowledge of God.[13] Augustine (354–430 AD) also found a "triple pattern [involving] an initial withdrawal from the sense world. . . . This is followed by an interior movement in the depths of the soul. . . . Finally, there is a movement above the soul to the vision of God."[14] The fifth-century theologian Pseudo-Dionysius the Areopagite identified the triad "of purification, illumination, and perfection or union (*katharsis*, *photismos*, *teleiosis* or *henosis*)."[15] This pattern of three ways of purgation, illumination, and

---

9. Louth, *Origins of the Christian Mystical Tradition*, 54–55.

10. Ibid., 59.

11. Gregory of Nyssa, *Commentary on the Song of Songs*, 202.

12. Louth, *Origins of the Christian Mystical Tradition*, 83.

13. Ibid., 102–103.

14. McGinn, *Foundations of Mysticism*, 233.

15. Louth, *Origins of the Christian Mystical Tradition*, 163; cf. McGinn, *Foundations of Mysticism*, 173–174.

union can be seen reappearing in the subsequent work of mystical theologians, most notably in the work of the great Carmelites of the sixteenth century, Teresa of Avila and John of the Cross.

These mystical theologians each in their own system of thought identified three phases of spiritual experience. Some have described these moments as occurring in a progressive sequence, roughly corresponding with the purgation or emptying required of a beginner, the illumination of the mind and heart of the proficient catalyzed by and through creation, and the ultimate culmination of transforming union with the divine. Imagine a short set of stair-steps representing the path of developing spiritual maturity. One moves from the purgative step, up to the illuminative step, and then finally to the topmost unitive step. Once a step has been achieved, one moves to the next, and once union with God has been attained, one remains in this state of divine union.

Our three moments of *kenosis*, *enosis*, and *theosis* bear some similarity to this classic schema of the purgative, illuminative, and unitive ways, but with several differences. First, our moments of *kenosis*, *enosis*, and *theosis* arise directly from the pattern and life of Jesus Christ as found in the Christ Hymn. As our lives and spiritual experience follow and reflect this pattern, we also follow and reflect the pattern of Christ. Second, these three moments describe and are rooted in relationship between humans and God. Each of these moments reveals a way we experience real and present relationship with God in the fabric of our lives. Finally, these three moments of *kenosis*, *enosis*, and *theosis* are free from the lock-step progression often implied by the classic schema. While there is a general "master" movement in our lives from *kenosis*, through *enosis*, toward *theosis*, as in the "V-shape" we found in the Christ Hymn, there is also a far richer way of viewing spiritual experience through these moments. We can identify these moments as literally moments in our lives, occurring not in sequential order, but arising intermittently as life is lived out.

We can view the occurrence of the moments of *kenosis*, *enosis*, and *theosis* as corresponding to a helix or spiral model rather than a lock-step progression. A helix model describes spiritual experience as falling along a spiral-shaped continuum rather than in a strictly sequential progression.[16] This model asserts that one may experience rounding moments of *kenosis*, *enosis*, or *theosis* without particular sequence, yet always spiraling in an

16. I am indebted to Rev. Luke Dysinger, OSB of St. John's Seminary in Camarillo for sharing this helix-based interpretation.

increasingly "upward" direction of developing spiritual maturity. Thus, one might experience any of these moments at any time, although such experiences differ in character, meaning and transformative impact at different times as the soul changes and develops. Divine effectiveness is unmistakably present in each of these moments.

Instead of a short set of three steps, imagine a soaring and brilliantly-colored spiral staircase with a strong central axis. As you progress up the spiral staircase, you are moving upward continually, always encountering new moments of *kenosis*, *enosis*, and *theosis*, not in any particular order, and sometimes the moments overlap and are experienced simultaneously. Sometimes you run into a rough dark blue patch of *kenosis*, sometimes life is tinged the rose-red of *enosis* in the experience of God through your neighbor's kindness and love. Sometimes all is brilliant and golden, and you bask in the experience of the divine touch of God—maybe even you glow golden too. Sometimes violet creeps into the climb as your *kenosis* and *enosis* merge together, and perhaps suffering combines with, and is tempered by, the experience of the divine in creation. Or perhaps in a sudden rainbow amid clouds, rain and sunlight, you experience all three moments at once. The rich canvas of your life unfolds as you ascend in your upward calling through the vibrant and oscillating moments of *kenosis*, *enosis*, and *theosis*.

The single constant of this helix-shaped staircase of spiritual experience is the strong central axis, God. God is always present, the linchpin in all human experience. Throughout scripture, God promises to be with us. Whatever we experience, even the worst *kenosis*, we know that God is present even if we do not feel that divine presence. When we can envision ourselves on that spiral staircase of spiritual experience, we can also see that the central axis upholds us and will never leave us. Even in the worst *kenosis*, when we are in intense darkness, we can trust that the strong and unmoving presence of God stands by us, promising, "Fear not, I am with you;/ be not dismayed; I am your God./ I will strengthen you, and help you,/ and uphold you with my right hand of justice" (Isa 41:10). Just as the central axis of the spiral staircase runs continually throughout the upward ascent, we remain in constant relationship with God in all of our moments of *kenosis*, *enosis*, and *theosis*.

Are you, like my dear friend Michelle, reading these three words and saying, "Laura, I love these three moments of divine-human relationship, but those three words are confusing. And I am a smart person!" The terms *kenosis, enosis,* and *theosis* are in Paul's language, and also in theological language from our Christian tradition. They have the specific meanings which I have developed. But I agree with Michelle that something a little more visual would be useful, even though less accurate. So to that end I turn to the poetic vision of Jessica Powers, a twentieth-century Carmelite nun. In stanzas of her poem "Beauty, Too, Seeks Surrender," she imagines God working to transform the surrendered soul as a sculptor might work on his stone:

> God's beauty, too, surrender seeks
> and takes in the will's lull
> whatever lets itself be changed
> into the beautiful.
>
> And so, Michelangelo
> has marked it out to be,
> since beauty is the purging of
> all superfluity,
>
> The yielded soul that lifts its gaze
> to harms past nature's claim
> expects to have experience
> of blade and file and flame.[17]

God is with us, and when God is with us, he is touching and transforming us. In the imagination of this poem, God the divine sculptor works transformation through use of blade, file, and flame. Each of these three tools is employed to transform the soul into beauty, specifically into divine beauty. Yet each of these three divine tools is different, and the action on the soul is different.

The blade as a metaphor for *kenosis* speaks of pain, loss, and suffering. It confronts us, perhaps corners us, perhaps drives us where we do not want to go, or separates us from ones we love. It can cut deeply, cause loss, cause hurt, or cause an emptying we could not have previously imagined. It can be unrelenting and merciless as steel. The blade may represent violence or outward physical suffering, or may be a hidden driving of knife in the heart, mind or soul. It may be a centurion's sword forcing us to a carry a cross, onto

---

17. Powers, "Beauty, Too, Seeks Surrender," 72. This quotation represents the last three stanzas of the poem.

the cross, or stabbing us in the side as we hang; it may be a gladiator's sword at our throats in the coliseum. The blade of *kenosis* is unmistakably in the dark shape of the cross. The blade may mow us down in bodily illness. It may twist cruelly in our relationships or emotional being. Yet paradoxically, sometimes the very same blade can end up working for our good. Job said, "Slay me though he might, I will wait for him" (Job 13:15). If we are in the midst of a blade experience, we can trust that it will not be without divine effectiveness. The direction we are forced into may ultimately yield unexpected blessings. Perhaps the pain we experienced equips us for empathic help of others. Or, the blade could cut away something toxic. Not unlike a surgical procedure, the blade's cut may be in the service of ultimately healing the patient. The blade may slice away parts of ourselves that we did not even know were cancerous, diseased, holding us back or keeping us from God. Or perhaps the divine effectiveness of the blade's wounding remains shrouded in mystery and we simply try to trust that God will take the slicing crown of thorns and in some miraculous way turn it into a crown of victory.

The file as a metaphor for *enosis* suggests a transformative tool which shapes gradually, at times smoothing our rough textures, and at other times providing us with details of character. The universe of people, places, and things in our individual lives provide steady contact points of *enosis*. Some of these contact points come to us in the gentle touches of a friend's encouragement, a hug at the right moment, the warmth of sunshine, or the sound of children laughing. Sometimes uplifting people and the beauty of creation motivate us and fill us with a longing to better ourselves. Teachers, writers, saints, mountains, and oceans can inspire and shape us; so can Special Olympic athletes, who use what they have to become the best they can be. Other contact points set up challenges which grate: the sandpaper of an argumentative person in the workplace, the sharp edges of a difficult family member, and all kinds of other unexpected bumps and spikes from the distressed, the depressed, the gravely ill, the dysfunctional, the manipulative, the negative, the self-absorbed, just to name a few. As you interact with these people and situations with peace and growing maturity, you are being contoured by the divine file, and perhaps even playing the role of a positive shaping file yourself. Sometimes a contact point may simply be encounter with difference or otherness. As the file works, we gain insight, understanding, compassion. We also may experience the file in encounter with creation, such as nature and animals. Observing the seasonal gains and losses of the fruit trees, the challenge of painting or hiking a difficult landscape, witnessing a sudden rainbow or even a simple butterfly can touch and shape us inside. One man I know experiences the touch of God when he surfs. My daughter has grown through the challenge of being a falconer and interacting with her hawk and his razor-sharp talons. The transformative file of God is at work in all these encounters with community and creation.

The flame as a metaphor for *theosis* evokes a divine flame embracing us to form and fire us into flame ourselves. A stone sculptor may use a torch to break away the top layer of rock. A sculptor of clay uses fire to harden, strengthen, and intensify the colors of her piece. A sculptor of metal such as bronze must use heat to melt and cast the metal. Yet our divine sculptor has far greater designs upon us. This flame seeks to transform us into its own likeness, flame itself. As John of the Cross explains, the divine Living Flame of Love acts upon our souls as fire acts upon wood. First the flame dries and then sets afire: "by heating and enkindling it from without, the fire transforms the wood into itself and makes it as beautiful as it is itself. Once transformed, the wood. . . . possesses the properties and performs the actions of fire: It is dry and it dries; it is hot and it gives off heat; it is brilliant and it illumines. . . . "[18] The Living Flame of Love touches us in order to transform us ultimately into flame, which in turn may give light and fire to others. As John suggests, this transformation involves a process of drying, catching fire, and burning well. The divine sculptor wishes not only to purge "all superfluity" with his tools, but to crown the soul with ultimate beauty—union with the divine. In our experience of the flame or *theosis*, divine fire ignites us into divinized flame.

If these metaphors of blade to describe *kenosis*, file to describe *enosis*, and flame to describe *theosis* help you to envision the transformative work of the divine sculptor, then imagine these tools at the ready in our following pages. The important thing here is that you begin to see these three moments everywhere, in your life, in the lives of others, corresponding, touching, changing.

For example, I felt the driving blade of *kenosis* when my friend Carolyn was diagnosed with pancreatic cancer, when I see her in physical pain, when I see her shedding weight and losing energy. My heart breaks under that blade when I hear the anguish in her voice as she speaks of her daughter. The blade cuts deeply when I see her in the hospital bed with tubes and lines in her devastated body. The blade crushes mercilessly as I see her fade

---

18. John of the Cross, *Dark Night*, 416.

slowly in her bed at home, her wasted hand in mine trembling violently even as she sleeps.

Yet the *enosis* I experience with Carolyn on the very same days are priceless to me. As she reaches out to me in her suffering, our friendship grows in such meaningful ways. We become the file of *enosis* for one another—she teaches me what it is to bravely push at the boundaries of life and death, and I give her a friend's loving hand to hold through that experience. The file of *enosis* whittles away at me wildly in our encounters, digging deeper grooves of compassion, endurance, patience, love, kindness, heartache, courage, tenderness and grief. Carolyn shares her experience with me, and it changes me.

The moments which become aflame with *theosis* in connection with Carolyn are chiefly the graced moments I experience in contemplative prayer and participating as a conduit of God's grace for Carolyn. These moments are unexpected, and they always fill me with joy in their fleeting suddenness and light. Often when I pray for and with Carolyn, including in our prayer group, I feel the sweep of the Holy Spirit in our petitions, the tilting of the rudder toward something that lies urgent and hidden in Carolyn's heart. "Yes, yes" she murmurs, and her face brightens as she feels the presence of God with us, touching us, transforming us through prayer. Sometimes on my drive to visit her I feel as though God tips a bowl of words into me for her. She listens, eyes alight, and I know that as I tip the bowl of words into her, God fills her with his presence, comfort, and light. In such moments, his flame catches fire in me, and then lights in her. In such moments we each are changed, we each are drawn ever closer into that bright flame of union with God.

Yet even as I describe them separately here, it is plain to see that each of my moments of blade, file, and flame are intertwined, each moment with one another, and also with Carolyn's *kenosis*, *enosis*, and *theosis*. My blade experiences of her suffering and the impending loss of my friend also closely connect to her *kenosis*. And this same *kenosis* shadows the moments of the file, the *enosis* we each experience, even as those very moments also may contain elements of fiery *theosis* for both of us. As we walk up our staircase of spiritual experience, the colors blend and merge, and sometimes echo and connect with the staircases of others.

The pattern and movement of the Christ Hymn of Philippians 2:6–11 provides the illuminating key to understanding not only the person and story of Jesus Christ, but ourselves and our own stories, as they are lived out in the pattern of Jesus Christ. Paul grasped that as Jesus emptied himself, lived among us, and was exalted by God the Father, so we also live out moments of self-emptying, experience of Christ-with-us in community and creation, and experience of confessing and expressing Jesus Christ in and through our words and actions. Just as the qualities of hiddenness and divine effectiveness are present in the "V-shaped" trajectory of Jesus Christ, so we as disciples of Jesus encounter those qualities in our own lives. Just as moments of *kenosis*, or emptying, *enosis*, or Christ-with-us, and *theosis*, or divine union, are present in the story and pattern of Jesus Christ, so they are also present and definitive in our spiritual experience and lives. While bearing some similarity with the classic "three ways" of purgation, illumination, and union, our three-way pattern differs in at least three crucial ways. First, the pattern of *kenosis*, *enosis*, and *theosis* arises from the shape of Jesus Christ as found in the Christ Hymn, and so the echoing pattern in our lives also imitates and expresses Jesus Christ. Second, each of these three moments is rooted in, and descriptive of, human-divine relationship. Third, these three moments not only describe a sequential "master plan" of increasing spiritual maturity, they also infuse our daily life in a non-sequential spiral-shaped continuum of spiritual experience, with God remaining at the center at all times.

Paul had discovered the key to his existence in Jesus Christ. He bequeathed this key to his Christian communities and to us, our own revelatory touchstone passed down in the form of the Christ Hymn, a text which marvelously unlocks and reveals the pattern and movement of not only Jesus Christ, but each one of us.

Chapter 4

Mark of the Messiah

The Living Christ Pattern in Paul

A FEW YEARS AGO I arrived at an after-school event at the park to collect my son, and began a conversation with another parent whom I had met recently through a mutual friend. As my son dashed by us intent on the slides, I said to her, "there's my son." She instantly replied, "I know about him. Of course he is your son. Who else could he possibly belong to?" Was she referring to the shape of his eyes, the curve of his smile, the expression of his words, or the contours of his heart? The clear implication was that my son, just by being himself, showed his belonging to me.

In a similar although much more profound way, we humans belong to something much greater and more infinite than ourselves, and when we accept and acknowledge it, we show our belonging to God in our behavior, our choices, our hearts, and sometimes even our physical appearance. Scripture reflects our belonging to God. In Hebrew scripture, we were created in the image of God: "God created man in his image,/ in the divine image he created him;/ male and female he created them" (Gen 1:27). God calls us his own: "I will take you as my own people, and you shall have me as your God" (Exod 6:7). Love seals the belonging: "With age-old love I have loved you" (Jer 31:3). Love desires the mark of belonging to the beloved: "Set me as a seal on your heart,/ as a seal on your arm;/ For stern as death is love,/ relentless as the nether world is devotion;/ its flames are a blazing fire" (Song 8:6). Our hearts become the metaphorical writing tablet of the divine, upon which we write God's commandments (Prov 7:3) and upon which God writes his law (Jer 31:33).

In the New Testament, God speaks to us and writes a pattern upon us in a new way: "In times past, God spoke in partial and various ways to our ancestors through the prophets; in these last days, he spoke to us through a son, whom he made heir of all things and through whom he created the universe" (Heb 1:1–2). Jesus Christ is the Word of God: "And the Word became flesh and made his dwelling among us, and we saw his glory, the glory as of the Father's only Son, full of grace and truth" (John 1:14). Jesus Christ is the revelation of God the Father (e.g., John 5:19). He himself became the way, the pattern impressed upon the hearts of believers: "I am the way and the truth and the life. No one comes to the Father except through me." (John 14:6). Jesus urged the expression of his pattern: "I have given you a model to follow, so that as I have done for you, you should also do" (John 13:15). The mark of belonging to the Messiah, then, is the impression of Jesus Christ and his pattern, upon our hearts, our souls, and our very lives. Crucially, we receive the gift of divine impression for the effective purpose of divine expression.

Paul expressed this imprint of the living Christ pattern radically and profoundly. Interiorly, Paul experienced relationship with, and the pattern of, Christ to such a degree that he felt that he lived in and through Christ: "I have been crucified with Christ; yet I live, no longer I, but Christ lives in me" (Gal 2:19–20). Even exteriorly, Paul felt that he carried the markings of Christ, perhaps in scars resulting from his physical suffering, "From now on, let no one make troubles for me; for I bear the marks of Jesus on my body" (Gal 6:17). In verses 3:5–15 of the Letter to the Philippians, Paul connects his life so intimately with Jesus Christ that he presents the account of his life, either consciously or unconsciously, after the pattern of the Christ Hymn. One scholar observes: "The autobiographical section of the letter, 3:4–11, is striking, not only for its content but for the fact, often overlooked, that it parallels the structure of the Christ-hymn. In so doing, it reinforces the thesis that Paul looks to Jesus Christ as *the* model for his own thinking and acting."[1]

Consider the text of Paul's autobiographical account in Philippians 3:5–15 as arranged here in the "V-shape" form, echoing the motion and moments of the Christ Hymn (Phil 2:6–11):

---

1. Hawthorne, "Imitation of Christ," 173; see also Dodd, "Story of Christ."

5   Circumcised on the eighth day, of the race of Israel, of the tribe of Benjamin,
    a Hebrew of Hebrew parentage, in observance of the law a Pharisee,

6   in zeal I persecuted the church, in righteousness based on the law I was blameless.

7   [But] whatever gains I had, these I have come to consider a loss because of Christ.

8   More than that, I even consider everything as a loss because of the supreme
            good of knowing Christ Jesus my Lord. For his sake I have accepted the loss of all
            things and I consider them so much rubbish, that I may gain Christ

9   and be found in him, not having any righteousness of my own based on
                the law but that which comes through faith in Christ, the righteousness
                from God, depending on faith

10   to know him and the power of his resurrection
                        and [the] sharing of his sufferings
                            by being conformed to his death,

11   if somehow I may attain the resurrection from the dead.

12   It is not that I have already taken hold of it or have already
                        attained perfect maturity,
                    but I continue my pursuit in hope that I may possess it,

13   since I have indeed been taken possession of by Christ [Jesus]. Brothers, I for
                my part do not consider myself to have taken possession.

14   Just one thing: forgetting what lies behind but straining forward to what lies ahead, I
            continue my pursuit toward the goal, the prize of God's upward calling, in Christ Jesus.

15 Let us, then, who are "perfectly mature" adopt this attitude.

Paul's autobiographical story reflects the same movement and moments we discovered within the Christ Hymn—the motion of descending and ascending, as well as the moments of *kenosis, enosis,* and *theosis.*

Paul begins his autobiographical account at the apex of a well-respected Jewish identity (3:4–6). He remarks on his respectable Hebrew ancestry as well as his observance of the law as a Pharisee (3:5), and his zealous persecution of the church in blameless adherence to the law (3:6). Yet Paul empties himself of this high state, declaring, "whatever gains I had, these I have come to consider a loss" (3:7)—a movement of descent and *kenosis* "because of Christ" (3:7). The descending movement continues in the next verse, as Paul "even consider[s] everything as a loss because of the supreme good of knowing Christ Jesus my Lord" (3:8). The next verse plummets further, as Paul definitively "accept[s] the loss of all things and [considers] them so much rubbish" (3:8). In the perhaps ultimate loss of his Pharisaic identity, Paul empties himself even of his former essential core and guiding compass, "righteousness of my own based on the law" (3:9). Paul's disclosure of his *kenosis* is radical and simple—he has been emptied of everything attached to his former life and identity.

For Paul, the point of the emptying of self is "that I may gain Christ, and be found in him" (3:8–9), a clear indication of *enosis*, being with and in Jesus Christ. Loss of righteousness based on the law is compensated or replaced by righteousness "through faith in Christ" (3:9). In the intimacy of the moment of *enosis*, Paul expresses the desire simply "to know him [Christ]," an aspiration expressed elsewhere in his letters, "I resolved to know nothing while I was with you except Jesus Christ, and him crucified" (1 Cor 2:2). *Enosis* for Paul goes beyond simply being with Christ, he participates and shares in the life, sufferings, and crucifixion of Christ. He wishes to partake in "sharing of his sufferings by being conformed to his death" (Phil 3:10). In an echo of the midpoint of the Christ Hymn, which is "even death on a cross" (2:8), the midpoint of Paul's autobiography is Paul's conformity to this very same death (3:10). Notice also that in an echo of the Christ Hymn, Paul's *kenosis* blends seamlessly into his *enosis*, with the moment of self-emptying becoming all but conflated with the *enosis* of sharing, a profound closeness and sharing even in self-emptying and death. Paul's expression of being with Christ, of his *enosis*, is deeply intimate and participatory.

In an ascending trajectory of transformative union, or *theosis*, Paul speaks of undergoing radical transformation through this deep identification with Jesus Christ. Through a participatory union of knowing Christ and his resurrecting power, Paul anticipates that he will "attain the resurrection from the dead" (3:11). For Paul, resurrection is about Christ's power to transform and change us into something like himself: "He will change our lowly body to conform with his glorified body by the power that enables him also to bring all things into subjection to himself" (Phil 3:21). Paul trusts in this ultimate transformation of resurrection because he *already* is experiencing dynamic and identity-shaping transformation in and through Jesus Christ. This is his *theosis*, his powerfully transforming participation in Christ, which happens both in the now for him, and yet also is to come for him, in a consuming and ever-increasing transformative union with Jesus Christ. This *theosis* or deeply participatory union with Jesus Christ (once again, notice the harmonious melding of the intimacy and sharing of Paul's *enosis* with the transforming union of *theosis*) experienced by Paul enables him to be increasingly conformed to the pattern of Christ. In verses 2:10–11 of the Christ Hymn, humans are enabled to confess and express Jesus Christ. The echoing response in Paul's parallel account confesses Christ and expresses Christ, in and through the transformed and transforming human Paul, according to an ascending pattern of God's upward calling in Christ.

In keeping with the deeply paradoxical way Paul experiences Christ and his cross, Paul describes this ascending transformative union in paradoxical terms. Paul explains that he has "been taken possession of" (3:12), or powerfully held in close relationship, by Jesus Christ; yet he simultaneously and paradoxically does "not consider myself to have taken possession" (3:13). Similarly, Paul has experience of *telos*, his purpose, his fulfillment, and his coming to perfection (3:15, the derivative word translated as "perfect maturity") in and through Christ; yet he says he has not attained it as yet (3:12, again "perfect maturity"). In the same sense that Paul has consistently called the attention of his readers to two alternative realities, one rooted in the earthly perspective and the other flowing from a heavenly perspective, Paul himself experiences two realities regarding his transformation in and through Jesus Christ. On the one hand, he is keenly aware of the punishing race he endures, and of his own fight to possess the "prize of God's upward calling in Christ Jesus," not yet attained. Yet he is also passionately in the grip of Jesus Christ, and his whole being conforms to, and is transformed in and through, his Lord. This intense present-moment experience of the transforming presence of the complete and perfect Jesus Christ in his life and his very being function to fulfill and complete him precisely in his present-moment incompleteness. Paul thus paradoxically experiences two realities—just as he says he is simultaneously not yet in possession yet possessed, he is also simultaneously unfulfilled and yet fulfilled in Jesus Christ, simultaneously incomplete yet completed in the embrace of the Complete.

Our metaphor of the magnet provides a simplified way to view Paul's paradoxical experience of *theosis*. In the last chapter, when considering the motion of the moments of *kenosis*, *enosis*, and *theosis* in the Christ Hymn, we envisioned Christ as a magnet swooping down and then rising up again, attracting and drawing up after it a trail of metal filings, which have become mini-magnets themselves. Now imagine Paul as one of those metal filings, filled by the power of the magnet drawing him, magnetized in his own right, yet relying totally upon the magnet for both the magnetization and the upward motion. In the same way that the metal filings are magnetized yet draw all their magnetic character and power from the magnet, Paul experiences *theosis* or divinization, a human "metal filing" becoming increasingly like the divine "magnet" empowering him, Jesus Christ. Paul expresses this dynamic: "I have the strength for everything through him who empowers me" (Phil 4:13). Analogous to Paul's paradoxical expression of his experience of *theosis*, Paul the metal filing is both held by the magnet yet does not have a hold on the magnet or its transforming power; he is both made very like the magnet in power and function, yet is not fully the magnet but relies upon the magnet. The metal filing can only be filled with the power of the magnet and become magnetized itself when it is in the magnetized grasp of the magnet. This describes Paul's experience of *theosis*, his transforming unity in and with Christ, a transforming unity which gives rise to "the prize of God's upward calling, in Christ Jesus" (3:14).

Paul recognizes the transforming divine shape of Jesus Christ within himself and declares Christ not only the source of his strength and identity, but the singular goal and prize of his life: "Just one thing: forgetting what lies behind but straining forward to what lies ahead, I continue my pursuit toward the goal, the prize of God's upward calling, in Christ Jesus" (Phil 3:13–14). There is a mutuality about this transformative experience of *theosis*; Paul is being touched, possessed, and transformed by the divine, but Paul is simultaneously reaching and striving upward toward his goal of "God's upward calling" in and through Christ Jesus. Moreover, Paul leaves everything else aside, and focuses single-mindedly and urgently on attainment of this goal. Fittingly, the ascending path of our "V-shape" comes to a culmination on this note of Paul's ascendant stretch to arrive at the prize of God's upward calling.

Yet it does not quite end there. Paul, ever the father of his communities, concludes his account of his experience of Jesus with all of its moments of *kenosis*, *enosis*, and *theosis*, with an instruction to them. Just as these three moments are Paul's key to God's upward calling in Christ, Paul wants us to know they are likewise the key for all followers of Christ. In an echo of the prelude to the Christ Hymn, verse 2:5, "Have among yourselves the same attitude that is also yours in Christ Jesus," Paul concludes his own autobiographical account by restating his exhortation, "Let us, then, who are 'perfectly mature' adopt this attitude" (3:15) of single-mindedly striving to follow Christ and his pattern. For Paul, the "attitude" of Christ Jesus which was fully expressed in the *kenosis*, *enosis*, and *theosis* of the Christ Hymn, are completely echoed and re-expressed in and through Paul's own "attitude" articulated in the moments of *kenosis, enosis,* and *theosis* of his autobiographical account. The two texts describe two sides of the same coin, and together they provide a magnificent roadmap for us.

In all of Paul's moments of *kenosis, enosis,* and *theosis* occurring in his autobiographical account in Philippians 3:5–15, the one constant and supporting center is divine relationship. Jesus Christ is with Paul in his *kenosis*—Paul is emptied and sustains loss for the very purpose of gaining Christ. His experience of loss is thus paradoxically counterbalanced by the gain of Christ. Paul's *enosis* is overwhelmingly filled with relationship with Jesus Christ, to the point of Paul wishing to share in everything with him, even his suffering and crucifixion. Paul's *theosis* is also chiefly characterized by relationship with Jesus Christ. Paul experiences intense and participatory union in his conformity to, and "possession" by, Christ, and strives with all his being for reciprocal possession of Christ. His life's goal focuses entirely upon the pursuit of "the prize of God's upward calling, in Christ Jesus" (3:14), which is attained in and through that very same participatory union with and in Christ.

This remarkable autobiographical echo of the pattern in the Christ Hymn indicates that Paul views Jesus Christ as the pattern of his own life in all its moments of *kenosis, enosis,* and *theosis.* We can identify the same master pattern in Paul's autobiographical account. Yet we can also detect the same helix or spiral-shaped pattern of moments of *kenosis, enosis,* and *theosis* occurring throughout Paul's life. This spiral-shaped pattern of spiritual experience falls across Paul's letters, a spiral staircase of God's upward calling in and through Christ Jesus. For Paul, the triune God is the strong central axis of this staircase. All of Paul's moments of *kenosis, enosis,* and *theosis* are connected to and stem from this divine relationship. In and through this relationship, Paul walks through these ascending moments of suffering, Christ-with-us in creation and community, and transforming unity—sometimes experienced as separate moments, sometimes merging together. Although these moments blend and meld in the vibrant spectrum of the staircase, we can also tease them apart and identify the separate elements of each moment threading throughout Paul's life.[2] Let us take a look at the colors of Paul's spiritual landscape as he renders it in his letters.

2. These moments may be identified separately, and simultaneously may be fused together in some combination. For example, with respect to the conflation of *kenosis* and *theosis,* Michael J. Gorman notes, "To be fully human is to be Christlike and thus Godlike in this kenotic and cruciform sense. Cruciformity, it turns out, is really *theoformity.*" Gorman, *Inhabiting the Cruciform God,* 37.

Paul knows the shape of the cross well. His multi-shaded inky *kenosis* appears on page after page of his letters to us. "You want to know about suffering for the sake of the gospel?" he seems to say. How about these raw details:

> Five times at the hands of the Jews I received forty lashes minus one. Three times I was beaten with rods, once I was stoned, three times I was shipwrecked, I passed a night and a day on the deep; on frequent journeys, in dangers from rivers, dangers from robbers, dangers from my own race, dangers from Gentiles, dangers in the city, dangers in the wilderness, dangers at sea, dangers among false brothers; in toil and hardship, through many sleepless nights, through hunger and thirst, through frequent fastings, through cold and exposure. And apart from these things, there is the daily pressure upon me of my anxiety for all the churches.[3]

Notice that Paul gives us a wide range of affliction here, of exterior and interior sufferings, of physical pain and mental anguish—sufferings inflicted by people, nature, bodily injury and deprivation, falsehood, hard labor, poverty and need, and mental and emotional pressure. Paul expects us to understand that each item of this list represents grave suffering. For example, when Paul was stoned, he was thought to be dead: "They stoned Paul and dragged him out of the city, supposing that he was dead" (Acts 14:19). Add to this list other moments of suffering by Paul: temporary blindness (Acts 9:8), emptying of self and identity (Phil 3:7–8), persecution (1 Thess 2:2, 15), ridicule (1 Cor 4:12), homelessness (1 Cor 4:11), imprisonment (Phil 1:13), physical illness (Gal 4:15), spiritual pain (2 Cor 12:7–8), laboring (Phil 3:16) and pouring out of self for the churches (Phil 3:17), and ultimately a martyr's death by beheading, according to church tradition. Paul considered himself "crucified with Christ" (Gal 2:19), suggesting that he considered all his self-emptying and suffering in conformity with, and in unity with, the crucified Christ (Phil 3:10).

Paul's embracing and crimson-tinged *enosis* threads throughout his letters as well. In fact, the letters are primarily motivated by *enosis*—Paul's relationship with Christ, and his love through Christ for his young Christian communities. The letters abundantly testify to Paul's intense experience of relationship with Christ, "who has loved me and given himself up for me" (Gal 2:20). Paul encountered the risen Christ in multiple visions (e.g., Acts 9:4; 2 Cor 12:1–7), and directed his entire being toward Christ,

---

3. 2 Cor 11:24–28.

desiring a total conformity to, and participatory sharing with, Christ (Phil 3:9–10). Yet significantly, for Paul, Christ extended beyond the person of Jesus Christ to include the church, each and every one of the followers of Jesus, who together function as the body of Christ: "we, though many, are one body" (1 Cor 10:17). They are to have the mind and attitude of Christ. They are to have different functions to support the body of Christ, just as the body parts all work together to make up and support the body (1 Cor 12:12–27). Paul understood that Christ was all but indistinguishable from those he loved, and so Paul's own love for Christ and his communities were intermingled and one: "how I long for all of you with the affection of Christ Jesus" (Phil 1:8). Paul expresses this love for and support of his communities repeatedly, and most particularly in connection with Christ: "my brothers, whom I love and long for, my joy and crown, in this way stand firm in the Lord, beloved" (Phil 4:1). Paul considered himself a loving and instructing parent to his young churches, "we treated each one of you as a father treats his children, exhorting and encouraging you and insisting that you conduct yourselves as worthy of the God who calls you into his kingdom and glory" (1 Thess 2:11–12). Here in Paul's *enosis* we can detect, as in his *kenosis*, elements of interior experience, primarily motivated by love, firing exterior experience, seen abundantly in the careful fostering of his communities. Paul's *enosis* is fueled and fired by love and relationship in and through the Lord.

Paul's gilt moments of light-drenched *theosis* occur in connection with his growing transformative unity with Jesus Christ. Once again, we can perceive these moments in Paul's interior and exterior experience. Interiorly, Paul experiences such a unity with Christ that he feels he has been taken hold of or possessed by him (Phil 3:12) and Christ lives in him (Gal 2:20). He perceives his very being as increasingly reflecting the pattern and image of Christ. In Paul's most potent statement of *theosis*, he considers the transformation toward likeness to Christ which he perceives in himself, and in others: "All of us, gazing with unveiled face on the glory of the Lord, are being transformed into the same image from glory to glory, as from the Lord who is the Spirit" (2 Cor 3:18). As we have seen, in keeping with this internal experience of transformation toward Christ, Paul depicts himself after the pattern of Jesus Christ, whether consciously or unconsciously. We also see this transformative unity playing out in Paul's external action and words, in examples both large and small. Paul confesses Jesus Christ in his proclamation of the gospel directly (e.g., 1 Cor 15:1–8) and with his

own added theological insight which reflects his experience of transformative unity: "For if we have grown into union with him through a death
like his, we shall also be united with him in the resurrection" (Rom 6:5).
Paul expresses his transformative unity with Christ through his words, actions, and very being. In fact, Paul expresses Christ himself, and the love of
Christ for his church. Even Paul's writing itself, his letters which have come
down to us, which are full of the confession and expression of Jesus Christ
through the Holy Spirit, have become more than Paul's words; inspired by
the Holy Spirit and expressive of unity with the Lord, they have become our
holy scripture, the Word of God.

We can perceive clearly that Paul did not simply experience *kenosis*,
enosis, and *theosis* in a rigid lock-step progression, but in a kaleidoscopic
tapestry of upwardly ascending and interwoven moments. Paul's *kenosis* of
suffering experiences occurred among his experiences of *enosis*, his love
for Christ and his communities, which also occurred amid his experiences of *theosis*, moments of such transformative unity with Christ that
Paul felt Christ lived within him. As Paul journeyed his vibrant spiral
staircase of spiritual experience, sometimes it was characterized by the
hue of one of these moments, sometimes by two, and occasionally even all
three of these moments came powerfully together. In fact, these moments
sometimes blend so beautifully together for Paul that they become hardly
distinguishable.

For example, in Philippians 2:17–18, we can detect all three of these
moments, even as we also marvel at the way they have become one for
Paul. Paul writes from prison and faces probable death for proclaiming the
gospel and fostering Christian communities. Yet his message to the Philippians is one of shared joy: "But, even if I am poured out as a libation upon
the sacrificial service of your faith, I rejoice and share my joy with all of you.
In the same way you also should rejoice and share your joy with me." Paul's
kenosis of suffering in prison and facing a sacrificial death melds seamlessly with his *enosis*, his love for Christ and his Body, the young Christian
communities, in his pouring out of self in their service; yet both of these
moments also merge flawlessly into his *theosis*, a transformative unity with
Christ so harmoniously expressed that he acts in the place of Christ, who
gave himself over as an effective and blameless sacrifice in love and faith.
Can you detect Paul's separate yet interwoven multi-hued strands of spiritual experience here? Paul indeed experienced each component powerfully
and separately: suffering and pain; love of Christ and communities; and

participatory union with Christ; yet in this moment for Paul they all join together in an interlocked whole of powerful Christian experience. Paul's life depicts the way these moments of *kenosis, enosis,* and *theosis* may occur both distinctly and fused together, as one ascends the vivid staircase of one's upward calling.

Paul was deeply aware of this distinctive pattern of Christ in all its moments of *kenosis, enosis,* and *theosis,* and realized that this living pattern manifesting in his own person and life was the key to God's upward calling in Christ Jesus. Because he recognized the pattern so profoundly in himself, he also seized upon a crucially important truth—just as he imitated or conformed to the pattern of Christ in and through these moments, each Christian was called to do so also. Christ offered the model for all Christians. Paul saw that he himself and other exemplary Christians offered the way *to imitate* the model of Christ. Paul's call to *mimesis,* or imitation, therefore runs throughout his letters.

Paul's call to *mimesis* occurs in the letters in three forms. First, Paul directs the community to imitate (as in 2 Thess 3:7, 9), or to be an imitator (as in 1 Cor 4:16; 11:1; 1 Thess 1:6; 2:14), or a fellow-imitator (as in Phil 3:17) of Paul or others. Second, Paul encourages his communities to follow the personal example of Paul or others, as in Phil 3:17 and 1 Thess 1:7. Third, Paul exhorts the community to be of the same mind or adopt the attitude of another (as in Phil 2:5; 3:15), or simply to do what they have "learned and received and heard and seen in me" (Phil 4:9). Paul consistently used these varying expressions of *mimesis* to urge his communities to imitate the model of Jesus Christ, and to take Paul and other Christians as examples of how to imitate Christ.

As twenty-first-century Christians, the idea of imitating Christ is familiar. Yet have you ever stopped to think about what that might mean in your own life? After all, although being like Christ as nearly as possible may be our goal, we are located firmly in our own bodies, times, places, and personhood. How can we be like Christ, or like Paul, who imitated Christ?

Sometimes in the summers I walk in a particular lane in Colorado, gorgeous in late summer beauty and for me full of the presence of God. The landscape on either side of this lane overflows with country wildflowers, grasshoppers, and little white butterflies fluttering among the grasses and flowers. In her writings St. Teresa of Avila used the metaphor of the silkworm to talk about transformation in Jesus—at first worms, we become cocooned in Jesus Christ, in which we die to our worm-selves and then emerge as transformed little white butterflies. The little white butterflies in the lane always reminded me of Teresa, and of my own hope to be transformed in and through Jesus. I wanted to become Teresa's little white butterfly, transformed in likeness to Jesus and closer to God. But one summer when I walked in the lane, looking for the little white butterflies, all I could find the entire length of the lane were little violet butterflies. The butterflies were beautiful, intensely purple, and made their home among the wildflowers which happened to be purple that summer. But I felt oddly frustrated that my beloved white butterflies had been supplanted by the violet ones, and kept looking in vain for the white ones.

I wanted to see the little white butterflies because for me a white butterfly was the only way to be Teresa's butterfly. Yet in that lane filled with flitting violet butterflies, God gently showed me that I am not a white butterfly, nor do I need to be. Rather, I am a purple butterfly. I am my own singular expression of the butterfly transformed in and through Christ. It is indeed my occupation to be the butterfly, yes. But it is also my vocation to express Christ through my particular personhood, to be the butterfly in the precise way God has made me and calls me, which in terms of butterfly wings, happens to be violet.

Our rather wooden English word "imitation," which sometimes carries implications of boorish copying or cheap knock-offs, simply fails to do justice to the richness of meaning behind the Greek word *mimesis* and its derivatives employed by Paul. *Mimesis* was a concept utilized by the ancients in the expression of human relationship with the divine. Study of the word *mimesis* suggests that the original meaning contained a more positive understanding of "bringing of something to expression, representation or portrayal"[4] which has been underestimated. One scholar, Willis de Boer, explains that Plato (ca. 428–348 BC) used the word *mimesis* to describe the relationship between the transcendent idea (divine) and the immanent object (human). For Plato, the transcendent idea is present in the immanent object by virtue of the *mimesis*, and conversely, *mimesis* allows the immanent object to participate in the transcendent idea. So *mimesis* includes the concept that God is present in us by virtue of our *mimesis*, and also the idea that humans may participate in the divine life in and through our *mimesis*. De Boer finds that Aristotle (384–322 BC) suggested that *mimesis* brings "the hidden potentialities and forces of nature to ordered and beautiful

---

4. De Boer, *Imitation of Paul*, 8.

expression."[5] Additionally, de Boer suggests that the first-century Jew Philo (20 BC–50 AD) utilized *mimesis* both to describe the Logos (Word) imitating God and, significantly, the effort of man to become like God.[6] So we can gather from these varied ancient usages of *mimesis* that the concept as it came down to Paul included the ideas of participation in the divine, expression of the divine, and human effort to became like the divine.

So when Paul calls on us to imitate him, the meaning and implications are far deeper than we first suspect. Paul urges us to participate in Christ, and express the Christ pattern in and through our individual being. Paul grasped that Christ left behind a map of our upward calling, in his very person and life, and he urgently desired to instruct his communities, and us, to perceive this marvelous Christ-shaped pattern of *kenosis*, *enosis*, and *theosis*, and to embrace and express it in each of our lives and our very selves. Paul understood that the shape of Jesus Christ spoke for itself, but that an example such as his own of conforming to this shape could assist us in sensing our own path to *mimesis*. After all, Paul expected *each and every one of us to strive to participate in this shape*. He did not call only the strong, or the gifted, or the brilliant, or the mighty. He called all of us, even, and perhaps especially, the littlest of birds.

But what exactly did Paul mean by his call to *mimesis*? What specific aspects of Paul, modeling Jesus Christ, are we to imitate? I would suggest that *mimesis* indicates an individualized adaptation of both interior and exterior aspects of the life of Paul, which involves self-emptying (*kenosis*), loving and ethical interaction (*enosis*), and transformation of the soul (*theosis*). Many have suggested that Paul meant for his communities to emulate his exterior ethical behavior, humble self-abnegation, and obedient conformity to Christ. But Paul, who experienced so much of Christ both interiorly and exteriorly, and cared so much about both the interior and exterior experience of his communities, meant to include *both interior and exterior experience* in his concept of *mimesis*. For Paul, interior love-charged conviction prompts exterior behavior. The interior experience gives rise to external expression; and the exterior experience expresses the interior Christian matrix. The two experiences inform and fire one another—we bring prayer, thought, and love to outward experience and outward experience back to prayer, thought and love.

5. Ibid., 6.
6. Ibid., 12–13.

Paul's words and actions so clearly spring from the source of his union, love, and commitment to Christ that it is natural for him to presume that those emulating him would, in that *mimesis*, draw from the same interior well of Christ. Some hallmarks of Paul's interior spiritual experience include: his emphasis upon and trust in prayer; reliance upon God's work in connection with interior change; expression of his desire to be in intimate relationship with Christ; and his profound interior identification with Jesus Christ. Accordingly, in his letters Paul also expresses concern about similar aspects of the interior lives of those in his communities, such as prayer, perception, thought, discernment, motivation, attitude, intentionality, desire, love, longing, joy, and peace. Two examples found in Philippians reveal Paul's careful attention to emotional state and thought. He encourages them to peace rather than anxiety through prayer, "in everything, by prayer and petition, with thanksgiving, make your requests known to God. Then the peace of God that surpasses all understanding will guard your hearts and minds in Christ Jesus" (Phil 4:6–7). The hearts and minds of the Philippians will be protected by peace granted through prayer—all of which occurs interiorly. Similarly in verse 4:8, Paul encourages the Philippians to holy thought: "whatever is true, whatever is honorable, whatever is just, whatever is pure, whatever is lovely, whatever is gracious, if there is any excellence and if there is anything worthy of praise, think about these things." Paul concerns himself with the interior state of his beloved Philippians to such a degree that he encourages the direction of their very thoughts.

Paul assumes that this Christ-centered interior state will give rise to exterior Christian morality and behavior. Social interactions, ministry, charitable efforts, ethics, and behavior should reflect the interior Christian love, discernment, and mind of Christ. For example, in the Letter to the Philippians, exterior *mimesis* includes proclaiming Christ out of love (1:15–16), fruitful labor (1:22), "sacrificial service" (1:25; 2:17), standing firm in one spirit (1:27, 4:1), perhaps suffering (1:29) and struggling (1:30), obedience (2:12), shared rejoicing (2:18), setting aside differences, coming "to a mutual understanding in the Lord" (4:2), and kindness shown to all (4:5). Paul expects that the behavior of the Philippians will be a match for the model they have in Christ: "Conduct yourselves in a way worthy of the gospel of Christ" (1:27).

For Paul, the interior and exterior aspects of *mimesis* flow together seamlessly. Perhaps this organic and effortless connection is best observed in Paul's commentary on love:

Love is patient, love is kind. It is not jealous, [love] is not pompous, it is not inflated, it is not rude, it does not seek its own interests, it is not quick-tempered, it does not brood over injury, it does not rejoice over wrongdoing but rejoices with the truth. It bears all things, believes all things, hopes all things, endures all things. Love never fails.[7]

Paul finds the connection between the interior experience of Christian love and the exterior expression of Christian love so innate that they cannot be separated in this passage. Christian love simultaneously shapes both the interior experience of the Christian, and forms her exterior actions. As we reflect and express the shape of the Christ pattern, we do so interiorly and exteriorly, yet our pattern is one of a unified expression of Christian love.

Paul experienced the pattern and mark of the Messiah Jesus Christ in his life and in his very being. Not only did Paul identify moments of self-emptying, or *kenosis*, Christ-with-us as experienced in creation and community, or *enosis*, and the confession and expression of Jesus Christ through transformative unity, or *theosis*, in the person and life of Jesus Christ as articulated in the Christ Hymn of Philippians 2:6–11, but he echoed and re-expressed these same three moments in his own autobiographical account as found in Philippians 3:5–15. Paul realized that the Christ pattern marked and shaped him as belonging to Christ, and further provided the upwardly ascending and spiraling pathway of his calling in Christ Jesus. But this map of the upward calling was not just for Paul. Paul urged his communities, and us, to recognize and facilitate this same Christ-shape in our individual selves and lives, and to hold on to this precious pattern as the singular path of our upward calling in Christ Jesus; for, "you shine like lights in the world, as you hold on to the word of life" (Phil 2:15–16). In finding expression of this pattern, Paul encouraged imitation of himself and other exemplary Christians. The *mimesis* Paul had in mind is participatory and expressive of Jesus Christ, is comprised of moments of *kenosis*, *enosis*, and *theosis* which fall along a spiral staircase of spiritual experience, and includes both the interior and exterior spheres of the individual. Paul implores each of us to hold on to this pattern, even those of us who consider ourselves little birds with a limited range of flight. The upward calling depends less upon the span of our wings and more upon the span of our hearts. After all, one who participates in Christ through the expression of his divine pattern reveals, simply by being himself, his belonging to God.

7. 1 Cor 13:4–8.

Chapter 5

Messiah, Expressed

The Living Christ Pattern in the Many

IN 1950, PABLO PICASSO contemplated how he might undertake to copy Diego Velázquez's famous 1656 painting *Las Meninas*. He reasoned that by changing the position of the characters in the painting, he would have to modify the light, and so his painting, while being a reinterpretation of *Las Meninas*, would also entirely be his own. In 1957 Picasso created a series of 58 paintings, each echoing and re-expressing in a completely new way the original *Las Meninas*. This series, now housed in the Museu Picasso in Barcelona, is a visual testimony to humanity's spirit of creative adaptation. In addition to Picasso's work, Velázquez's *Las Meninas* has also inspired quite a number of other imitative re-creations, including works by Edgar Degas, Salvador Dalí, and even a delightfully stylized grouping of sculptures by Manolo Valdés. Each of these artists, and many others as well, captured and re-created something of *Las Meninas*, while simultaneously expressing a fresh and singular interpretation.

When we undertake the imitation or *mimesis* of Christ, we render it on our own canvas of individuality. Each one of us is a singular creation of God, located in our own time and place, born of our own parents, with our own DNA, with a given gender and culture, in particular environmental circumstances, with our own heart, mind, and physicality, and endowed with our own particular interests, abilities, and talents. When Paul urged *mimesis*, he did not have in mind an identical replication of Jesus Christ which would give rise to a line of rigidly-duplicated sameness among Christians. Rather, just as Paul experienced the expression of Christ in and through his own particular life, circumstances, and being, Paul envisioned a rich and wide-ranging array of expressions of Jesus Christ in and through the many who love him.

A quick look at what the scholars have to say on this subject will help illustrate this point. Some have suggested that Paul was employing *mimesis* as a crafty and political power dynamic to enforce "sameness."[1] But most of the others who have weighed in on this subject reject this assertion, finding that *mimesis* involves repetition which always includes difference, and moreover, "our practice of repetition itself constitutes the 'identity' of that which we are endeavoring to repeat."[2] A.K.M. Adam emphatically asserts that efforts to mechanically copy "the particularity of Jesus (or Paul)" deny "the particularity of our own identities or vocations."[3] His suggestion is that disciples of Jesus, as exemplified by the saints, express faithfulness to the gospel and the example of Jesus and Paul through differential repetitions, which fulfills the promise of Jesus that others would come after him and do greater things.[4] Stephen Fowl also finds that "[t]he imitation called for here is not a wooden sort of identical repetition, but a 'non-identical repetition' based on analogy, examples of which are seen in [Phil] 1:19–26; 1:27—2:4; 2:12–18; 2:19–30, and 3:2–16."[5] Angela Standhartinger takes a similar position: "In Philippians, the instigation to creative adaption goes so far that Paul can say, 'and if you think differently about anything, this too God will reveal to you.'"[6]

1. Castelli, *Imitating Paul*, 15, 119–21. See also Marchal, *Hierarchy, Unity, and Imitation*. Utilizing a feminist rhetorical approach, Marchal suggests that the use of rhetoric by Paul in Philippians functions to create a dominant and preeminent position of authority; Marchal, *Hierarchy, Unity, and Imitation*, 204–205. *Contra*, see Copan's response to Castelli, finding her analysis to be "an exercise in mono-dimensional reading that ended up excluding evidence to the contrary." Copan, *Saint Paul as Spiritual Director*, 218; and Park: "In sum, while Castelli has raised provocative and important questions concerning the power relations in Paul's mimetic injunctions, her work neither offers a substantive challenge to traditional readings nor a progressive contribution to biblical studies: the multiple inconsistencies within her model of mimesis, the misappropriation of the underlying philosophy and weak support of textual evidence (Hellenistic and biblical) render her work unpersuasive." Park, *Submission Within the Godhead*, 80–116.

2. Adam, "Walk This Way," 30.

3. Ibid., 32.

4. Ibid.

5. Fowl, "Christology and Ethics in Philippians," 148 (noting that the phrase "non-identical repetition" belongs to John Milbank; see Milbank, "Can a Gift Be Given.").

6. Standhartinger, "Join in Imitating Me," 431.

So we may gather from these observations that *mimesis* includes the idea of *creative and individualized adaptation* of the Christ pattern. Christ gave us the pattern, and Paul gave us the insight that we should imitate this particular Christ pattern, and one example of what *mimesis* would look like as expressed in and through the individual called Paul of Tarsus. As A.K.M. Adam notes, the saints provide an incredibly rich tapestry of the range of the Christ pattern, which is indeed an expansive continuum of completely individual, varied and creative expressions of the Christ shape.

When I say the word "saints," do you immediately put them into a different category than yourself? This little bird sometimes does. In fact, let me share something that once happened to me when I was sitting at my desk, writing something about the great saints. I said to God in anguish, "My heart wants to soar and do great things for you, but I will never be like St. Anthony, or St. Francis, or St. Benedict, or any of these great saints who did such incredible things, and levitated, and healed, and. . . . " Through my tears as I looked out my window, I saw a small bird shoot up from one side of the window, ascending and crossing my window with a single melodic note of birdsong, as I simultaneously inwardly received a response to my prayer, "No, you will not be them. But you are my little bird." Later, when I read St. Thérèse's account of the little bird, which I shared with you in chapter 1, I realized that this was exactly the kind of little bird I am, and that many of us are. Thérèse had the insight that God may make saints of the smallest of us, even in our own ordinary circumstances and lives. In fact, it is precisely in our smallness and ordinariness that he calls us to be his own little birds. So, little birds, take heart. God tells you—*you*—that you are his little bird, and that you are capable of reflecting this lovely pattern of Christ in exactly the delightful and particular way which you have been called to express.

So when we use the word "saints" here, we mean human beings who have found their own distinctive way of expressing the pattern of Jesus Christ in and through their hearts, their interactions, their statements, their undertakings; in short, in and through their very being and lives. Each is given their own unique time, place, circumstances and personhood, and through that individuality each may discover his or her own particular way of expressing the Christ pattern, or his or her own *mimesis*. In finding our own way, as Paul instinctively knew, it is helpful to see the many ways the Christ pattern has been expressed through others.

To this end, let us take a look at how that Christ pattern has been expressed in some of the lives of those who have gone before us, and in the lives of some of our contemporaries. There are literally hundreds of thousands of examples of holy and faithful people who have found their own way of expressing the Christ pattern, and I hope that after we look at a few examples, you will begin recognizing the pattern in not just the lives of the few, but the many. So let us trace the Christ pattern in the lives of some of our brothers and sisters—looking with more detail at the lives of Francis of Assisi and Mother Teresa, and examining in less detail a contemporary family living in Charlotte, North Carolina. It is my hope that as we move from the more distant in time and extraordinary life of Francis, to the closer in time to us and the perhaps more ordinary lives of others, that you will more closely connect their particular ways of expression of the Christ pattern with your own path, which lies open before you, waiting to be rendered in an exquisite and individual expression of your own.

We take St. Francis of Assisi as our starting point because Francis himself had a profound sense that his life followed the "footprints" of Jesus Christ. Francis was born in Assisi, Italy in 1182, the son of a wealthy middle-class cloth merchant, Pietro di Bernardone.[7] As a youth he led a boisterous life of carousal, followed by a brief military service which was brought to an end through a vision he had during illness in which a voice urged him to serve God rather than man. Francis embarked on a life of giving to the church and service of the poor, and soon experienced a second vision while praying before an image of the crucified Christ above the alter in the small neglected church of San Damiano. The image of Christ spoke to him, saying: "Francis, don't you see that my house is being destroyed? Go, then, and rebuild it for me."[8] Francis, filled with new purpose, set out to literally repair the church of San Damiano. It was only years later that Francis realized that the vision contained a more expansive meaning. In the meantime, his father was furious at Francis for selling some of the family goods to fund church repairs. His father had him brought before the bishop's court to recover the money, and to assert his authority over his son. But instead of returning to his father, Francis stripped naked, and handed over both the money and his clothes. In this dramatic way, Francis made a statement that he would rely on his Father in heaven rather than his earthly father.[9]

Following this break with his family and turning to the life of a hermit, Francis experienced a transformational moment. He encountered a

7. Brown, *Little Flowers of Saint Francis*, 13.

8. Spoto, *Reluctant Saint*, 44.

9. Ibid., 52–54.

colony of lepers on his return journey from a pilgrimage on foot to Rome. Instead of avoiding them, which would have been his former impulse, he approached the most lame of the group, embraced him, and spoke words of comfort. Francis experienced tremendous grace in this moment, and on his return to Assisi he began to minister to lepers.[10] On February 24, 1209, Francis was powerfully impacted by the gospel of the day's mass, specifically Matthew 10:9–10. Francis felt that this passage revealed the specific way of life to which he was called by God, one of itinerant preaching and poverty.[11] Within weeks he was joined by three companions in his way of life, which developed first into a band of holy men, and eventually into the Order of Friars Minor. In 1212 Francis set Clare of Assisi over a Second Order of enclosed nuns, which became the Order of Poor Clares.[12] Nine years later Francis established a lay Third Order, the Order of Brothers and Sisters of Penance. Francis also exhibited a special love for nature, through which he experienced the presence of God. He regarded all aspects of nature and the animals as creations of God, and thus his brothers and sisters in God.[13] Many accounts attest to his preaching to birds, taming a fierce wolf of Gubbio, and other instances of kind interaction with animals.

Francis lived a simple life firmly rooted in the gospel, deliberately living out his life according to the example of Jesus. He was well known for his humble yet effective preaching, and his constant emphasis on peace as well as his efforts to bring peace to communities. Beginning in 1220 Francis experienced a period of spiritual darkness in connection with increasing bouts of malaria and blinding trachoma, and tensions which arose within the Order regarding the rule of life.[14] The earliest biographers of Francis report that in September of 1224 while praying on Mt. Alverna, Francis encountered an angel and was imprinted with the stigmata, the five wounds of Christ in his hands, feet, and right side.[15] He lived for two more years, during which time he battled various illnesses and blindness, and composed the *Canticle of Brother Sun*. His early biographers attribute many miracles

10. Ibid., 57–59.

11. Ibid., 67–68.

12. Brown, *Little Flowers of Saint Francis*, 14–15.

13. Spoto, *Reluctant Saint*, 203.

14. Brown, *Little Flowers of Saint Francis*, 16–17; Spoto, *Reluctant Saint*, 166–173; 188.

15. Brown, *Little Flowers of Saint Francis*, 17; Spoto, *Reluctant Saint*, 190–194.

to Francis, both before and after his death on October 3, 1226. Francis was canonized by Pope Gregory IX just two years after his death.[16]

Even in this highly abbreviated account of his life, we can detect the outline of the master Christ pattern. In his first coming to God, Francis experienced *kenosis*, an emptying of his former way of life. Francis lost his desire to indulge his whims for pleasure and a military life. He lost his identity as the carousing youth, and the son of the wealthy cloth merchant. He gave up the affluence and security of that identity, literally stripping himself naked in a dramatic expression of his *kenosis*. He stripped himself inwardly and outwardly in total trust and reliance upon God alone. Francis experienced *enosis* profoundly in his embracing encounter with the leper, which led him to embrace and serve other lepers. His master *enosis* played out further in the inception of his community of Friars Minor, which touched and inspired the lives of many, and led to the institution of the Second and Third Orders. We can also detect *enosis* in Francis' great love and concern for nature and animals. Finally, as Francis conformed himself ever more closely to Jesus Christ in his way of life, his actions, and his words, he experienced *theosis*, a divine transformative unity which manifested in his life and very being. Francis echoed the gospel and the life of Jesus in countless ways, but in particular in his poverty, his preaching, his care for the marginalized, his love for all, and his steadfast service of God. Accounts of his preaching resulting in conversion of the many, and reports of healing as a result of his intercession are just two of numerous ways he confessed and expressed Jesus Christ. The stigmata represent an outward sign of Francis' passionate conformity to, and divine unity with, Christ.

Yet we can also perceive a magnificent and many-hued helix of spiritual experience winding throughout the life of Francis. Francis endured dusky-edged moments of *kenosis* along the ever-ascending spiral staircase of his journey to God. He emptied himself of his former way of life. His chosen way of life embraced *kenosis* on a daily basis—abject poverty often meant he was without shelter, hungry, and subject to the elements. He suffered miserably from illness throughout his adult life, most notably from malaria, gastrointestinal pain, and trachoma which all but blinded him; he also underwent leaden spiritual darkness. Francis emptied himself of personal safety, concern, and health as an itinerant preacher. Yet, here the staircase glows indigo with intertwine of *kenosis* and *enosis*; Francis pours himself out, but in favor of another, in an embrace of his brothers and sisters in God.

16. Brown, *Little Flowers of Saint Francis*, 16–17.

Many of the recorded moments of Francis radiate the rose of full-flowered community. The legend of Francis and the wolf of Gubbio provides an excellent example of the *enosis* of Francis. Francis, aroused to compassion for the community of Gubbio, went out into the wild to search for the wolf which had terrorized the town, attacking both flocks and humans. Yet Francis, so in touch with God as expressed in and through all creation, recognized in the wolf his own brother creature. According to his biographers, Francis chastised the wolf in the name of Jesus Christ for his murderous acts, and then engaged in a gentle and fair peace negotiation with the wolf, which was ratified in the midst of the townspeople of Gubbio.[17] The wolf essentially became a member of the community of the town, as the people provided food for him, and he lived peacefully among the people; he became a living reminder to them of the peace of God brought to them through their brother Francis. The *enosis* of Francis necessarily flowed into the *enosis* of the people of Gubbio, who experienced the presence of God in and through community—here, the human Francis; and creation—in this case, the peaceful camaraderie of their newfound wolfish friend.

Yet this moment also contains golden-edged hints of *theosis*, for Francis echoed and expressed Jesus Christ in his peace-making endeavor. In fact, the life of Francis was filled with moments of *theosis*, moments in which Francis was so closely united with Jesus Christ that he seemed to be a living expression of Christ in the world. The deep participatory union Francis experienced with God found expression in many outward actions and signs. His care and concern for the marginalized, his healing touch, his devotion to prayer, his wisdom, and his constant witness to the kingdom of God all provide unmistakable glimmers of his growing union with Christ. In the case of Francis, perhaps the most dramatic outward expression of *theosis* was the stigmata. For his contemporaries, there could be no greater sign of participatory union with Jesus Christ than the physical manifestation of the five wounds of Christ.[18] For us today, the stigmata reported so long ago still provides a powerful expression of the "marks" of Christ seen in and through Francis of Assisi—an echoing sign of the passion of Christ revealed through Francis' participatory union with Christ (*theosis*), yet also containing elements of suffering in the crucified wounds (*kenosis*) and providing a sign of Christ-with-us (*enosis*).

---

17. Ibid., 88–91; 320–322.
18. Spoto, *Reluctant Saint*, 190–196.

Perhaps the most beautiful and potent moments in the life of Francis occurred in the kaleidoscopic concurrence of *kenosis, enosis,* and *theosis* together. In one such pivotal moment, Francis encountered the leper whom he treated with love and embraced. The moment is simple yet profound. In it we find the *kenosis* of personal risk and humility. Francis overcame his natural revulsion for the contagious and diseased leper on the margins of society. He not only emptied himself of personal concern for health and safety, but he poured out his love upon one considered an outcast and a reject. In the same moment we find the *enosis* of love and compassion for another in and through Christ. Francis experienced the meaning of Christian community in a way he had never before in the moment of intense love and compassion for the least of humanity, the diseased, impoverished, and dying. Finally, we can identify in the very same moment the *theosis* of Francis, who became Christ to the leper. Christ himself encountered and touched lepers, healing them in compassion. In embracing the leper, Francis drew from the well of his participatory union with Christ, a well of transformative grace which empowered and made possible his echoing expression of Christ. This synchronicity of *kenosis, enosis,* and *theosis* together was such a memorable and transformative moment for Francis that he made a point of recounting it in his short deathbed testament.

Another such moment occurred as local violence broke out in Assisi in 1226. Although near death, Francis summoned the two enemies to a courtyard. Francis was carried out on a pallet and sang with great effort a new verse of his *Canticle of Brother Sun*, which included the phrase "blessed are those who endure in peace."[19] As a direct result of this, the rivals agreed on terms for a peace treaty. The *kenosis* of Francis is found here in his effort despite great physical suffering, and his outpouring of original song. The *enosis* is clear also—he was motivated to plead for peace for the good of the community, and in addition he gave the community the gift of another verse of the already-cherished *Canticle*. Finally, the *theosis* of Francis radiates in his impassioned plea as a peacemaker, paraphrasing the words of Jesus spoken in the Sermon on the Mount (Matt 5:9).

Moment after moment of the life of Francis renders the vivid upwardly ascending spiral of his spiritual experience. The descending and ascending movement of *kenosis, enosis,* and *theosis* in his life's master pattern is apparent, just as we can also spot the daily moments of *kenosis, enosis,* and *theosis* playing out in all their unexpected confluences of darkness and brilliance.

19. Ibid., 206–207.

The content of Francis' particular expression of the Christ pattern is sometimes surprisingly stark and simple, sometimes breathtaking in audacity and love, and consistently a creative adaptation of the life and person of Christ. Imagine Francis as one of our metal filings, once isolated in self-centered dissipation, yet eventually encountering and attracted by Christ the magnet. As Francis our metal filing is drawn into the magnetic field of Christ, he is reoriented in polarity and character, reconfigured to reflect the shape and pattern of Christ even as he retains his own individual structure. In this powerful magnetization or divinization, Francis is drawn up after Christ, joining a chain of "magnetized" followers of Christ, each completely unique yet bearing the hallmarks of the One who empowers them. Francis of Assisi was indeed completely distinctive in his *mimesis* of Christ, and yet we can detect the unmistakable Christ pattern which was so eloquently expressed in and through his life.

Are you beginning to envision that magnetic chain of divinized followers of Christ? As we know from playing with magnets and paperclips as children, a magnetized metal filing is capable of drawing up another filing after it as well. Then in turn, that magnetized filing may draw another yet another filing, and so on. The Christ magnet is the singular source of attraction and power, and yet the attraction and power of Christ can be transmitted through other magnetized metal filings. That is precisely why we are attracted to Christ, yet we also are attracted to the same Christ in and through the lives of those creatively expressing the Christ pattern. So each person expressing the Christ pattern in her or his own way also contains the potential to transmit the pattern of Christ to others. As Paul of Tarsus became expressive of Christ, his example and words inspired countless others to follow Christ. Centuries later, Francis of Assisi, surrounded by "a cloud of witnesses" (Heb 12:1) such as Paul, journeyed his own path and became expressive of Christ, in turn inspiring countless others to follow Christ. One of those inspired by Francis of Assisi seven centuries after his life was Saint Teresa of Calcutta, better known to most of us as Mother Teresa.

Teresa of Calcutta was born Anjezë Gonxhe Bojaxhiu on August 26, 1910 in Skopje, Republic of Macedonia.[20] At the age of twelve she felt a call to the religious life. At eighteen she left home for Ireland to join the Sisters of Loreto. She took her first temporary vows on May 24, 1931, and took the name "Teresa" in honor of Thérèse of Lisieux.[21] She began teach-

20. For a detailed account of Mother Teresa's life, see Spink, *Mother Teresa*.
21. Ibid., 12, 14.

ing at the Loreto convent school in eastern Calcutta in India, and took her final vows on May 24, 1937.[22] She served at the school as a teacher and later headmistress for almost twenty years in total, and apparently never expected to serve otherwise. But all that changed on September 10, 1946, when she experienced what she later described as "the call within the call."[23] While traveling on a train from Calcutta to the Loreto convent in Darjeeling for an annual retreat, Teresa heard the voice of Jesus asking her to leave her teaching service and go into the slums of India to help the poor, the sick, the dying, and the abandoned children. After a year and a half, in January of 1948, permission was finally granted to her to leave the convent and pursue this calling. On August 16, 1948, Teresa departed the convent for a night train with only her ticket and five rupees, wearing a simple white sari with a border of three blue stripes.[24]

After several months of basic medical training, she returned to Calcutta and started an open-air school for children in the Motijhil slum. By October 1950, twelve others had joined her in her work, and she received canonical approval for her congregation, the Missionaries of Charity. In 1952 she successfully applied to the local government for the grant of a building for use as a home for the dying.[25] In the ensuing years, her congregation established a leper colony, an orphanage, medical clinics, family clinics, and a nursing home. In 1965 her congregation received recognition from Pope Paul VI in the form of a Decree of Praise, which prompted Teresa to expand her work internationally.[26] The Missionaries of Charity expanded first into Venezuela, then Rome, Tanzania, and Austria. In the 1970s the congregation steadily established houses and foundations in Africa, Asia, Europe, and the United States. Over the years the order also expanded to include both active and contemplative brothers and sisters; associated branches were established for priests, lay Catholics, and non-Catholics.[27] The Missionaries of Charity and its branches were becoming a widespread and well-known resource of help for "the poorest of the poor."

Teresa herself became the focus of international attention, and received a series of awards, prizes, honorary degrees and citizenships in

22. Ibid., 16–17.
23. Ibid., 22.
24. Ibid., 31–32.
25. Ibid., 53–54.
26. The Holy See, "Mother Teresa."
27. Spink, *Mother Teresa*, 103–149.

recognition of her humanitarian work; in 1979 she received the Nobel Peace Prize. Although she had some detractors, for the most part the figure of Mother Teresa had become—to Christians and non-Christians alike—a living symbol of goodness. She was viewed as someone truly living out her faith, and moreover, living the kind of life we most admire—a 1999 Gallup poll declared her to be the most admired person of the entire twentieth century.[28] Yet the most remarkable thing about this life of faith is that it was lived out during a profound spiritual darkness. The publication of her private letters after her death leaves no doubt that privately Teresa encountered intense darkness in her spiritual life for almost fifty years.[29] Yet she faithfully continued to execute the request made of her by Jesus. Despite her very prolonged interior experience of emptiness and darkness, as well as an intense and often unrequited yearning for God, Teresa faithfully worked day in and day out to serve the poorest of the poor and to be an expression of God's love in the world. Beginning with a heart attack in 1983, Teresa's health began to decline. After another heart attack and surgery to receive a pacemaker in 1989, additional cardiac problems in 1991, a broken collarbone in 1996, followed by malaria and failure of the left ventricle, she stepped down on March 13, 1996 from her position as head of the Missionaries of Charity. She died on September 5, 1997. India honored her with a state funeral in gratitude for her services to the poorest of the poor, and she was mourned across the globe.[30] She was beatified by Pope John Paul II on October 19, 2003, and canonized by Pope Francis on September 4, 2016.[31]

The life of Mother Teresa provides us with an extraordinary modern example of someone living out a life of faith which reveals the pattern of Christ we have been considering. We can trace her "master pattern" of *kenosis, enosis,* and *theosis* by following the rhythm of her life: a descent downward in her gradual giving over of herself to Christ, culminating in her first steps in the Calcutta slums; and the gradual rise upward as her mission took root, provided help and care to the poorest, and spread across the world. Teresa took all her steps in faith. There were the steps of *kenosis*—leaving her mother and sister at age eighteen; entering the Loreto convent; her profession of vows; her service of teaching; her abandonment of all the safety and security of Loreto in favor of a life of service on the streets

---

28. Newport, "Mother Teresa Voted by American People as Most Admired Person."

29. Mother Teresa, *Come Be My Light.*

30. Spink, *Mother Teresa,* 283.

31. Ibid., 298; Kington, "Mother Teresa Declared a Saint."

of Calcutta; her poverty and exposure; and the vast uncertainty of the risk she was taking. There were the steps of *enosis*—the teaching in the convent school; the desire to help the poor not simply with their physical needs but with their need for human dignity and love; the day by day encounter with the broken and dying people of Calcutta; the emergence of her order, and the many who were moved to join her in her effort of love; and the worldwide support she ultimately received. There were also the steps of *theosis*, slowly emerging from the strands of her *kenosis* and *enosis*—as she navigated these steps of self-giving and Christ-with-us in community, she began to reflect something more than just the person of Teresa, or even of Mother Teresa. She began to be a beacon of light in the world, a reflection of Jesus Christ in our contemporary times. When she ministered to the least, to the children, the dying, the abandoned, and the lepers, she became, as Paul would say, no longer Teresa, but Christ in Teresa.

As with all of our lives, Teresa's life was not only characterized by this falling and rising pattern, but also fraught with the ups and downs of the daily moments of *kenosis*, *enosis*, and *theosis* occurring in no particular order, yet always in relationship with God, and always spiraling upward as she walked her "spiral staircase" of spiritual experience. The moments, at times, contained the midnight ink of total self-giving or spiritual darkness, such as when she departed her Loreto convent in the middle of the night to embark on her mission in the slums with five rupees in her pocket, or when she experienced the absence of the presence of God. Yet other moments unexpectedly glowed sunrise red with the love of her neighbor, such as when she tucked an abandoned and emaciated boy into her apron with love,[32] or experienced the arrival of new postulants, ready to dedicate their energy and love to her mission. Her moments of *theosis* occurred sometimes unexpectedly with her full knowledge, as when the railway car blazed golden in a sudden union with Jesus, who had an important proposal. But they also sometimes occurred without her notice, when others experienced the love of Jesus Christ through her, or perhaps without her full understanding, when the Jesus Christ of her union was the one on the cross uttering the agonized cry of "Eloi Eloi lema sabachthani?" or "My God, my God, why have you forsaken me?" (Mark 15:34). In those moments of union with the crucified Christ, her *theosis* was also her *kenosis*.

Although there are many moments in Teresa's life which could illustrate the confluence of *kenosis*, *enosis*, and *theosis*, I would like to give you

---

32. Spink, *Mother Teresa*, 15.

an example from a simple everyday occurrence, a gesture of love which could happen in your own day. A woman in my parish named Eileen told this story from the pulpit one Sunday, about how she, as the secretary for the archbishop of Los Angeles, frequently received calls from the front door of the administrative building from people who claimed to be Mother Teresa (as well as Jesus, God, and so on; you get the idea). Once she received a call from someone who claimed to be Mother Teresa, only to discover upon her entrance that she was in fact Mother Teresa, paying an unexpected visit to the archbishop. Eileen immediately apologized that the archbishop was not there. But then something happened that Eileen said she will never forget. It was, she explained, as if Mother Teresa never even meant to see the archbishop at all that day, but smiled widely at her, exclaimed, "Eileen!" and gave her a hug, an embrace full of love. Even long after Mother Teresa had left, Eileen felt powerfully moved. She felt that she had been touched by Jesus through Mother Teresa's embrace.

In that simple yet powerful moment, Teresa had taken the opportunity to give of herself, a gift which ended up being a cherished faith experience for Eileen. Perhaps Teresa expected the archbishop; perhaps she did not. But she knew that her expectation was completely irrelevant. What was relevant was the providential opportunity which presented itself, an opportunity to give of herself, and to pour out love (*kenosis*). The recipient of her gift of love, Eileen, was a human being who in that moment felt unable to give Mother Teresa what she at least ostensibly had come for, time with the archbishop. Mother Teresa undoubtedly encountered Eileen not as someone who could or could not provide her with something or someone, but as simply a person loved by Christ, her present community in Christ, her Christ-with-us—and her embrace was the ultimate expression of the love of Christ expressed in and through community (*enosis*). The very same moment illustrates the *theosis* of Mother Teresa, expressed so well by Eileen: the embrace felt like the love of Christ given in and through the person of Mother Teresa.

Consciously or unconsciously, Teresa cultivated the ability to see the effectiveness of God even in situations which appeared disappointing, fruitless, dark or painful. She connected her experiences so closely with her relationship with God that she was able to find the link of even her darker moments of *kenosis* with moments of *enosis* or *theosis*. This may seem at first blush to be an outrageous claim regarding a woman now famous for her profound and prolonged spiritual darkness. Yet the evidence of her ability to connect her personal darkness (*kenosis*) with Christ-with-us in community (*enosis*) and transforming union (*theosis*) is present in her life and her writings. Moreover, when Teresa connected her personal darkness with Christ-with-us in community or transformative union, she inevitably discovered *a hidden effectiveness in what she was currently experiencing.* Let me provide two examples of how Teresa's life has something to teach us about putting on our specially-crafted glasses, the lens of the cross, to perceive a hidden and effective reality.

Teresa's first sojourns onto the streets of Calcutta were exhausting and difficult, and threatened to derail her mission. In her diary she wrote,

> Our Lord wants me to be a free nun covered with the poverty of the Cross. Today I learned a good lesson. The poverty of the poor must be so hard for them. While looking for a home I walked and walked till my arms and legs ached. I thought how much they must ache in body and soul, looking for a home, food and health. Then the comfort of Loreto came to tempt me. "You have only to say the word and all that will be yours again," the Tempter kept on saying. . . . Of free choice, my God, and out of love for you, I desire to remain and do whatever be your Holy will in my regard. I did not let a single tear come.[33]

Teresa suffered the *kenosis* of wandering the streets of Calcutta without home or comfort. But instead of viewing her *kenosis* in a vacuum and making a choice to avoid it at all cost, she connected it to Christ-with-us in community—the poorest of the poor, the people she was called to serve. She made the jump from her day of suffering to their daily suffering, and how it was precisely her day of suffering which fueled her understanding of their plight and her motivation to live out her calling to assist them. Her *kenosis* suddenly took on a new and rich meaning when joined to her *enosis*. Moreover, she was also able to perceive another layer of meaning in her experience. She realized that her *kenosis* was also connected to her personal transformation and union with Christ. Would she accept the "poverty of the Cross" in union with Christ or would she return to the Loreto convent? She overmastered tears by perceiving that her *kenosis* was likewise joined intimately with her *theosis*—she saw that her personal transformative union in and with Christ involved joining him freely in the poverty of his cross.

What could have remained hidden in the misery of her day (*kenosis*) was uncovered when Teresa thought of those suffering on the streets of

33. Ibid., 37.

Calcutta (*enosis*) and of her transforming union with Christ (*theosis*). Suddenly the profound effectiveness of the day of suffering became clear. There was not simply one reality of homelessness, aching arms and legs, and conflict about her mission. There was a second reality also to be perceived, one of new insight into the suffering of those she was called to assist, and into her growing union with the Christ of the cross.

Teresa's later years of intense spiritual darkness posed a parallel interior dilemma on a radically soul-searing level. Now the *kenosis* was not simply one day of aches and longing for a home, but years of spiritual emptiness and longing for God, a prolonged and excruciatingly painful sense of the absence of God. As she entered more fully into her calling as a "nun covered with the poverty of the Cross," she experienced not only the physical poverty of the crucified Christ but his spiritual poverty as well—the sense of abandonment by God.

> Lord, my God, who am I that You should forsake me? The child of Your love—and now become as the most hated one—the one You have thrown away as unwanted—unloved. I call, I cling, I want—and there is no One to answer—no One on Whom I can cling—no, No One.—Alone. The darkness is so dark—and I am alone.—Unwanted, forsaken.—The loneliness of the heart that wants love is unbearable.[34]

Teresa wrote these private and anguished words in a letter to her spiritual director in 1959, words pouring from her heart almost against her will, but written in obedience to God himself: "Why He wants me to tell you all these I don't know.—I wish I could refuse to do it."[35] These words stand as an impassioned confession of her simultaneous love of God and intense sense of abandonment by God, and are words which powerfully and personally echo the agonized cry of Jesus from the cross, "My God, my God, why have you forsaken me?"[36]

Even as Teresa struggled through this persistent darkness, she slowly began to uncover a connection between this terrible interior *kenosis* and her *enosis*, the poorest of the poor she was called to serve. With the help of a priest who counseled that the interior darkness was connected to her calling, she perceived that she was experiencing what her unwanted and

---

34. Mother Teresa, *Come Be My Light*, 186–187.

35. Ibid., 186.

36. Mark 15:34; Matt 27:46.

unloved poor experienced daily.[37] Just as she had experienced the exterior aches and homelessness of her poor, now she was experiencing the interior emptiness and pain of the unwanted and unloved, and the hopelessness of those who did not have Jesus to light their way in the darkness. As the editor of her private letters later observed: "Her darkness was an identification with those she served: she was drawn mystically into the deep pain they experienced as a result of feeling unwanted and rejected and, above all, by living without faith in God."[38]

Having made this connection, Teresa was empowered to further connect her *kenosis* with her community in Christ, her *enosis*: she imparted it to her religious sisters as a vital insight regarding their shared charism as Missionaries of Charity. In the general letter to her sisters written in July of 1961, Teresa wrote:

> My dear children—without our suffering, our work would just be social work, very good and helpful, but it would not be the work of Jesus Christ, not part of the redemption.—Jesus wanted to help us by sharing our life, our loneliness, our agony and death. All that He has taken upon Himself, and has carried it in the darkest night. Only by being one with us He has redeemed us. We are allowed to do the same: all the desolation of the poor people, not only their material poverty, but their spiritual destitution must be redeemed, and we must have our share in it. . . . Yes, my dear children—let us share the sufferings—of our poor—for only by being one with them—we can redeem them, that is, bringing God into their lives and bringing them to God.[39]

The link between her *kenosis* and her *enosis* had remained hidden from her for years, yet when she finally was able to detect the connection between her spiritual darkness and her *enosis*, her poor and her religious sisters, she could also perceive the effectiveness—she was able to be "one" with her poor on a spiritual level, and teach her sisters to do the same. Moreover, this new insight helped her to endure her own spiritual darkness, because she could look beyond the reality of her interior suffering to a second reality in which God's work was being very effectively accomplished through her union with the poor's "spiritual destitution" and her consequently insightful guidance of the Missionaries of Charity.

37. Mother Teresa, *Come Be My Light*, 214–216.
38. Ibid., 216.
39. Ibid., 220.

Intimately tied with Teresa's discovery of the hidden *enosis* being served through her *kenosis* was an equally hidden *theosis*. For many years Teresa was not only pained by her spiritual darkness, but highly confused by it. She wanted only God, why did God give her all but himself?[40] When she finally received the good counsel from her priestly spiritual director to associate the suffering with her calling, she was able to not only connect it to her *enosis*, but also to her *theosis*—she realized that she was actually united with Christ in her very suffering. In overwhelming relief she wrote to her director:

> I can't express in words—the gratitude I owe you for your kindness to me.—For the first time in this 11 years—I have come to love the darkness.—For I believe now that it is a part, a very, very small part of Jesus' darkness & pain on earth. You have taught me to accept it [as] a "spiritual side of 'your work'" as you wrote.—Today really I felt a deep joy—that Jesus can't go anymore through the agony—but that He wants to go through it in me.[41]

Things were not as they had appeared to be. She was not alone and abandoned by the God she loved so much. Teresa had been given the gift of insight—of at last seeing her situation through the specially-crafted lens of the cross of Jesus Christ. There was a paradoxical and hidden reality underlying her spiritual darkness: she was so united with the crucified Christ that she experienced the agony of his sense of abandonment. She was united with him precisely in her sense of isolation.

Even before she could fully understand the paradox of these two realities pressing upon her, she experienced them paradoxically. Words written to her spiritual director in 1960 reveal the "contradiction" of the two realities she experienced:

> Heaven from every side is closed.—Even the souls that drew me from home, from Loreto as if they don't exist—gone is the love for anything and anybody—and yet—I long for God. I long to love Him with every drop of life in me—I want to love Him with a deep personal love.—I can't say I am distracted—my mind & heart [are] habitually with God.—How this thing must sound foolish to you because of its contradiction.[42]

---

40. "Why does He give all these [awards] but Himself? I want Him, not His gifts or creatures." Ibid., 237.

41. Ibid., 214.

42. Ibid., 202–203.

On the one hand, she felt all was lost, that heaven was closed to her, that she was alone and in great pain. On the other hand, she felt impassioned love and longing for God, and her mind and heart were habitually with God. The editor of her private letters points out the paradox of her daily situation: although "the very pillars of her life—faith, hope, love—had disappeared. . . . At the same time, paradoxically, she clung steadfastly to the faith she professed, and without a drop of consolation, labored wholeheartedly in her daily service of the poorest of the poor."[43] Before she was even cognitively aware of the underlying effectiveness of her *kenosis*, or how it connected to her *enosis* and *theosis*, or even how the two realities were both real and simultaneously present, she was experiencing the paradox. She held her suffering and isolation in one hand, but she also held her faith and love of God in the other hand. She experienced both of these realities, and her trial was located in the discrepancy or distance between the two realities. Yet she chose to live out of only one of the two realities, the reality of her faith and love of God.

Just knowing that we have a choice, that we retain the control to choose which hand, which reality we focus upon and follow, makes all the difference. Do you remember my dear friend Carolyn struggling with the horrific last stages of pancreatic cancer? Once when I went to visit her I found her in a tired bundle of misery, her big eyes staring out at me in total hopelessness. Everywhere her thoughts went, everywhere she looked, all appeared to be loss, death, pain, darkness, and suffering. As it happened, on my drive over to see her, Mother Teresa and her amazing ability to hold both those realities, one terrible and dark, the other joyful and light, came to me. As I sat with Carolyn and Mother Teresa's story spilled out of me to her, her eyes filled with tears of what I recognized as relief, hope, and even joy. "That helps so much," she told me. "I had only been able to hold on to one at a time. But to know that I can hold both at the same time, that I can hold on to the light even when it's all dark—that helps so much." I came to realize later that Mother Teresa, her life, and her *kenosis*, had given yet another beautiful gift to one dying.

Teresa's life and its participation in the Christ pattern also gives to you and to me, as we learn to discern how the pattern of *kenosis, enosis,* and *theosis* can be reflected in an individual and her life. "But that's *Mother Teresa*," you are thinking. "What about someone more ordinary? What about someone who is not a nun, someone today who has a family and a job?"

43. Ibid., 170.

Just as there are countless examples throughout the history of Christianity of those following the example of Christ in their own unique *mimesis*, there are countless examples today, all around you, in ways both small and nearly invisible, and big and breathtaking. I'll bet right now you can think of at least one person living today who reflects Christ and his goodness to you. When you think about that person, can you detect aspects of her or his giving over or loss of self (*kenosis*)? Can you uncover how that person's *kenosis* might be tied to her or his Christ-in-community (*enosis*)? Finally, can you perceive that person as being a sign or ambassador of Christ in the world through being so closely united with Christ (*theosis*)?

Len and Nicole Clamp provide an example of how "ordinary" people may live out of an extraordinary sense of following the example of Christ. Len and Nicole were high school sweethearts who married and moved to Charlotte, North Carolina in 2001. They began to discern that God was calling them to a particular way of expressing Christ. As Len explains, "Nicole knew early on that God was calling her (she later informed me that He was calling us) to do something special with needy children."[44] In 2009 the couple began to foster children through an organization called Carolina Family Connections. They did so specifically out of a desire to follow Christ: "We began fostering to follow Jesus' call to care for orphans . . . never intending really to adopt as we wanted to have children of our own."[45] Yet "God had a different plan. After fostering 4 wonderful babies (all medically fragile), Grayson came to us at 2 months old (direct from the hospital . . . direct from having open heart surgery). Grayson was born with a condition called CHARGE . . . leaving him with a heart defect, no hearing, and no sight in his left eye."[46] The Clamps adopted Grayson in 2010, and the next year Nicole gave birth to a son Ethan.

Despite Grayson's lack of auditory nerves in either ear, at eighteen months he received a cochlear implant, which was eventually determined to be non-beneficial. Through that process he became a patient of Dr. Craig Buchman at University of North Carolina. Dr. Buchman offered the Clamps the opportunity to place Grayson in an ABI (auditory brain implant) trial. In April of 2013, Grayson became the first child in the United States to receive an ABI. The device was activated on May 21, 2013, and little three-year-old Grayson heard his father's voice speaking to him for the first time. The

44. UNC School of Medicine, "The Grayson Clamp Family Story."
45. Ibid.
46. Ibid.

Clamps shared the moment of their child hearing for the first time with the media, and the unforgettable image of Grayson's response to sound played on the news channels and on the internet, allowing the world to become a witness to, in the words of Len, "the miracle work God can do through faithful parents and expert physicians."[47] As of this writing, Grayson not only can hear, but has begun to recognize words and even speak.

Len and Nicole could have fostered Grayson and not adopted him as their own child. Yet they chose to adopt him, specifically in response to the invitation of Jesus Christ to care for orphans, to welcome little children. Their *mimesis* of Jesus gives full flower to these words. They welcomed Grayson into their family as their own child. In choosing to be parents of Grayson, Len and Nicole gave of themselves in a profound way. Their *kenosis* was not only the choice to adopt and raise a child with special needs, but to permanently alter the landscape of their own family dynamic on a daily basis. But Len and Nicole were not just looking at the *kenosis* part of the equation when they made the choice. They were looking at Grayson in love. Who would raise Grayson? Who would pour out love on this child? The Clamps made their decision in the *enosis* of seeing Grayson as their Christ-in-community. Jesus said "whoever receives one child such as this in my name receives me" (Matt 18:5). The Clamps welcomed Grayson in the name of Jesus and after the pattern of Jesus, specifically because Grayson was loved by Jesus and precious in the eyes of Jesus, and so also loved and precious to them. Finally, the Clamps were choosing to follow Jesus and his words, and thereby choosing a transformative path in union and likeness to Christ, *theosis*. They were stepping into Grayson's life to provide the love and care that Jesus wished for him—they were becoming the heart and hands of Jesus to provide little Grayson with a home, love, and a family. In the same way that Francis became no longer Francis but Christ in Francis when he embraced the leper, and Mother Teresa became no longer Teresa but Christ in Teresa when she cared for lepers and abandoned children, the Clamps also became more than just Len and Nicole when they welcomed Grayson into their family. They became a living and daily outpouring of Christ's love on a medically-fragile child in need of parents.

This confluence of *kenosis*, *enosis*, and *theosis* as the Clamps walked the path of obedience and imitation of Christ was not without its effectiveness. Grayson received not only the gift of love, parents, a brother, and a home, but also, miraculously, the boy born deaf and even missing auditory nerves

47. Ibid.

received the gift of hearing. In a contemporary story of "the miracle work God can do through faithful parents and expert physicians," we can detect yet another special way that the Clamps confessed and expressed Jesus Christ. We glimpsed Jesus in Francis of Assisi declaring those blessed who endure in peace, and in Mother Teresa when she embraced the abandoned, sick, and dying in the slums of Calcutta. Now we glimpse Jesus also in the story of the Clamps: "He makes the deaf hear and the mute speak" (Mark 7:37).

Just as the body of Christ has many parts, and all the parts have different yet necessary functions, we Christians are simultaneously a whole yet comprised of many individuals called to many different and necessary ways of *mimesis*. Mother Teresa had her particular calling of founding the Missionaries of Charity and serving the poor of Calcutta; the Clamps had their calling of adopting Grayson. Thérèse of Lisieux discovered that her vocation was simply to love, and let every act of love, even the very smallest act, be done as an expression of love for Jesus. Dietrich Bonhoeffer, a German Lutheran pastor and theologian (1906–1945), wrote *The Cost of Discipleship* and lived that theme out by returning from the United States to Germany in order to be in solidarity with Christians there during the war; he was executed by the Nazis for his involvement in an anti-Hitler plot. Jim Elliot, a Christian missionary (1927–1956), went to Ecuador for the purpose of evangelizing the Huaorani people; after he and three other missionaries were killed in the attempt, his wife Elisabeth Elliot (b. 1926) went to live with the Huaorani and carry on the effort of Christian evangelization. Jessica Powers, a twentieth-century Carmelite nun (1905–1988), had a particular calling to write deeply evocative Christian poetry. Mary Clarke (1926–2013), a twice-divorced Beverly Hills mother of seven, founded the Servants of the Eleventh Hour and lived the last three decades of her life known as Mother Antonia, "the prison angel" of the notoriously dangerous La Mesa Prison in Tijuana, Mexico. My friend Jan is called to powerful intercessory prayer; my friend Kate is called to build enduring bridges of community between our church and our neighboring synagogue. The rich tapestry of Christianity reveals *mimesis* simple and complex, startling and seemingly mundane, on the world stage and hidden in the ordinary. The ways of faithfully pursuing the pattern of Jesus Christ in our collective *mimesis* are as many and varied as we ourselves are.

Yet the pattern remains. Even as we look to the almost endless variety of expression of the pattern, the particular hallmarks of the Christ pattern are the reliable constant: in each example of *mimesis* we find the outpouring of self in *kenosis*; the connection with Christ-in-community in *enosis*, and the transformative union of confessing and expressing Christ in *theosis*. If we examine more deeply, we may also uncover an undeniable effectiveness in the *mimesis*—perhaps initially hidden, yet powerfully present. As we observed in the case of Mother Teresa, often when the moments of *kenosis*, *enosis*, and *theosis* can be connected, a hidden effectiveness of the *kenosis* (and indeed all the moments) presents itself. *Mimesis* also likely contains the double edge of two realities—one of darkness and loss or suffering, the other of light and gain. The trial of the Christian lies in the discrepancy, or difference between, these two realities. Like Christ, like Paul, like Francis, like Teresa and so on, we have a choice of which reality governs for us. When we connect our suffering or loss to our Christ-in-community and our transformative ability to confess and express Christ, we begin to perceive that graced "second reality" of light and gain over against the present darkness.

You also figure in this tapestry of Christian *mimesis*. You also have your own completely unique location in time and space, and possess your own particular set of personal characteristics. You alone possess the potentiality of expressing the Christ pattern in your own completely individual way. Only you can bring the Christ pattern to your particular form of expression in your life, both interiorly and exteriorly. Your particular heart, your specific gifts, your circumstances, your sense of how God calls you, where you are being led—these things all provide the singular substance of the "you" ready to be rendered on the divine canvas in an utterly unique creative adaptation of the Christ pattern. Picasso portrayed with paint; you will bring Christ to expression with the hues and tints of living flesh, beating heart, loving embrace—the inhale of daily life and the exhale of divinely-patterned yet singular grace.

Chapter 6

Targets to Arrows

Divine Transformation

SEVERAL YEARS AGO I ventured with my younger daughter into a local shopping mall which just had undergone a massive expansion. She was four years old, and we held hands as we walked deeper into the seemingly endless labyrinth of stores in search of gifts, and then in search of the way back. Twisted around in the corridors and wondering where to find a map, I said aloud, "I am lost." My daughter turned her little sunny face up to me and said immediately, "I am not lost, Mommy. I am with you."

When we are on that sweeping and sometimes seemingly endless spiral staircase of our spiritual experience, moving in and out of ink and rust, turbulent blackness and placid sky blue, obscure gray and shimmering sunlight, we often wonder where we are and what it all means. But the wisdom of a child often reminds me that the key point is less about these questions, and more about *who* is with us in the very place we stand. Wherever we find ourselves on that staircase, there is one certainty—God stands beside us, in uninterrupted and loving relationship with us. God promises to be with us always—he is the unmoved hawk, with us on days of glorious blue sky, and equally with us in any and every hailstorm we encounter.

In fact, that promise to be with us is a golden thread running throughout salvation history and sacred scripture. It is the consistent word of encouragement given to those in uncertainty, to those asked to do something they do not feel able to do, to those who are fearful or discouraged. The message is often like that found in Isaiah: "Fear not, I am with you;/ be not dismayed; I am your God./ I will strengthen you, and help you,/ and uphold you with my right hand of justice" (Isa 41:10). With such words the Lord encouraged Isaac (Gen 26:24), Jacob (Gen 46:3–4), Moses (Exod 3:12), and many others. In Joshua, we have the Lord actually commanding Joshua to be strengthened and encouraged as he holds fast to the promise of the Lord to be with him as he walks his path: "I command you: be firm and steadfast (also translated as strong and courageous)! Do not fear nor be dismayed, for the Lord, your God, is with you wherever you go" (Josh 1:9). Joshua may have confidence that wherever he goes, God will be with him. The fact of God's presence promises effectiveness—regardless of whatever dark or dangerous circumstance he may encounter, Joshua will attain the goal of gaining possession of the promised land.

This message is carried on in a new and profound way in New Testament scripture: God comes to be with and save his people in the person of Jesus Christ. The author of the gospel of Matthew sees the birth of Jesus as the fulfillment of Isaiah 7:14, "All this took place to fulfill what the Lord had said through the prophet: 'Behold, the virgin shall be with child and shall bear a son, and they shall name him Emmanuel,' which means 'God is with us'" (Matt 1:23). In Matthew we also have the resurrected Jesus proclaiming, "And behold, I am with you always, until the end of the age" (Matt 28:20). These encouraging words which promise the continued presence of God with us are also the last words of the gospel of Matthew.

The promise of divine presence may be interpreted to include many elements, such as divine protection; fruitfulness; salvation from destruction, especially eternal salvation; the transformation and restoration of landscape and human beings, effectiveness in an undertaking, assurance of divine leading or guidance; victory; and bestowal of blessings and joy. There is something inherently alive, powerful, dynamic and effective in the presence of God with us. When God is with us, things grow, change, transform and are restored. For Paul, this divine transformation is specifically toward the likeness and image of Jesus Christ: "All of us, gazing with unveiled face on the glory of the Lord, are being transformed into the same image from glory to glory" (2 Cor 3:18). Paul sees our relationship with God as charged with effectiveness to transform us ever toward the divine pattern. As we make efforts to echo and imitate the Christ pattern in both our interior and exterior *mimesis*, our divine partner works in us gently in and through moments of *kenosis*, *enosis*, and *theosis* to touch and transform us moment by moment, step by step, "from glory to glory."

Our spiral staircase of spiritual experience is electric with this transformative effectiveness. God stands beside us as a strong central axis, constantly connected to us. God upholds and empowers us, and in each and every moment of relationship with us, each and every step on the staircase, the divine presence may touch and transform us, whether by lightning bolt or imperceptible current. As we move up the staircase, our progressive transformation catalyzes our progressive advancement in spiritual maturity, according to the general "master" movement in our lives from *kenosis*, the emptying and stripping away of all manner of things and attachments which separate us from God; through *enosis*, the experience of the divine in and through all creation and particularly in our experience of communities and nature; and ultimately toward *theosis*, our ever-progressing transformative union with God. These three master movements describe our general progression through the spiritual life, as in the "V-shape" pattern we explored in the Christ Hymn in chapter 3, in Paul's life in chapter 4, and in the lives of St. Francis and Mother Teresa in chapter 5. Simultaneously, as we also examined in each of these chapters, we experience a rich continuum of transformative spiritual experience through all the moments of *kenosis* (moments of darkness, emptying or loss), *enosis* (moments in which we experience the divine in and through creation), and *theosis* (moments in which we experience a oneness or union with God) which play out in our lives, in all the minutes and days and intervals of life—in the infinitesimally small and the vast, in the hidden and the laughably obvious, the simple smile and the complicated drama, in the whisper and the thunderclap. These moments of *kenosis*, *enosis*, and *theosis* occur without sequence, and may be experienced separately, two overlapping together, and sometimes the confluence of all together at once—*and all are charged with divine effectiveness*. God sequences these moments as he wishes, knowing precisely our interior landscape, and just what effective touches will heal and transform us toward increasingly greater likeness to the Christ pattern and divine union.

Yet even as we can know that these moments of divine-human relationship—*kenosis*, *enosis*, and *theosis*—are also moments of transformative effectiveness, certainly we will also experience the limits of our own human understanding of just what God might be doing in any given interval. As the Psalmist says, "I was stupid and could not understand;/ I was like a brute beast in your presence./ Yet I am always with you;/ you take hold of my right hand" (Ps 73:22–23). We must acknowledge from the outset that we simply cannot grasp the divine mind, even as we completely trust in God's work in us. "For my thoughts are not your thoughts,/ nor are your ways my ways, says the Lord./ As high as the heavens are above the earth,/ so high are my ways above your ways,/ and my thoughts above your thoughts" (Isa 55:8–9). We are the finite, even as we are privileged to stand at the edge of the Infinite.

Moreover, the transformative touches of God in and through these moments of *kenosis, enosis,* and *theosis* are sometimes known to us and sometimes hidden from us. The reasons why they may be hidden from us are many and mysterious, as mystics and spiritual theologians throughout the ages attest. For example, St. John of the Cross explains that the presence and touches of God may be hidden from us because we experience God as in a "dark night" of the soul or spirit, in which the brilliance and light of God are so great that they appear to us as a blinding and painful darkness. Yet this darkening has its own effectiveness, as the saint explains:

> [E]ven though this happy night darkens the spirit, it does so only to impart light concerning all things; and even though it humbles individuals and reveals their miseries, it does so only to exalt them; and even though it impoverishes and empties them of all possessions and natural affection, it does so only that they may reach out divinely to the enjoyment of all earthly and heavenly things, with a general freedom of spirit in them all.[1]

The divine effectiveness underlying the darkness may be the hidden work of stripping the individual of certain attachments which separate her from God, or healing the deepest parts of the self in order that the person may be more prepared for union with God. St. Teresa of Avila suggests that God may hide his graces from individuals even as far advanced in the spiritual life as in the sixth mansion of her *Interior Castle*, explaining that in this the person advances beyond mere intellectual reflection regarding humility, "for the experience of having suffered through it, having seen itself totally incapacitated, made it understand our nothingness. . . . For in this state grace is so hidden . . . that not even a very tiny spark is visible."[2] She also describes this intense experience of humility as a necessary and effective precursor to advancement to the seventh mansion of union with God.[3]

St. Ignatius of Loyola (1491–1556) describes another type of situation in which the presence and touches of God may be hidden from us: we may be undergoing a movement of spiritual desolation in which our

---

1. John of the Cross, *Dark Night*, 412.
2. Teresa of Avila, *Interior Castle* (Kavanaugh), 364–365.
3. Ibid., 365, 378, 397, 424.

spiritual experience is overshadowed by feelings of sadness, disquietude and discouragement. The person may feel abandoned by God in this state of desolation. The hallmarks of a spiritual desolation are spiritual confusion, discouragement, anxiety and disturbance—we are under spiritual attack by the enemy.[4] In this case, all of our spiritual experience is colored by our experience of spiritual desolation. Yet even in this spiritual desolation God conducts his effective work in us: Ignatius views spiritual desolation "as a 'lesson,' that is, as an experience able to impart spiritually valuable insight, [which] intimates why God may permit the enemy to visit us with this trial. Ignatius understands that when we faithfully resist spiritual desolation we 'learn' spiritual lessons highly useful for our spiritual journey."[5]

In yet another example of why God may hide his presence and grace, the French Jesuit Fr. Jean Pierre de Caussade (1675–1751) suggests that the touches of God may be hidden from us because the soul may unconsciously take credit for all the graces granted it by God, which defeats the positive transformative work of God by miring the person in pride. Those in the midst of God's transformative work "are unable to perceive a gift of God in themselves without running the risk of debasing and corrupting it by falling back, however imperceptibly, into self-complacency; they thus appropriate to themselves the grace of God."[6] De Caussade concludes that "[t]his leads [God] to hide almost all his gifts and graces from us."[7] Along similar lines, de Caussade suggests that God may give gifts and graces and then unexpectedly take them away. At some point the gifts may be restored once more "in a better form,"[8] once the person has experienced that the gifts do not arise from, or are not possessed by, themselves, but bestowed upon them by God: "The loss of the gift serves to take away its ownership. Ownership taken away, the gift is restored a hundredfold."[9]

These examples point to a few of the many productive though mysterious reasons why we humans sometimes may not be able to perceive the presence, much less the transformative touches, of God. Yet mystics such as John of the Cross attest to the assured effectiveness of these transformative touches, even in what we perceive as divine absence, darkness

---

4. Gallagher, *Discernment of Spirits*, 62–68.

5. Ibid., 68.

6. De Caussade, *Self-Abandonment to Divine Providence*, 286.

7. Ibid.

8. Ibid., 287.

9. Ibid.

or pain. In some ways it is far easier for us to accept that God is touching and transforming us through our moments of *enosis*—our experiences of Christ-in-community and through our interactions with individuals which shape us toward the Christ pattern—and through our moments of *theosis*—those experiences in prayer or in any situation in which we experience union with the divine. The challenge for us is to trust in the transformative effectiveness of the divine even when it is completely and radically hidden from us in any of these three moments, but particularly in our moments of *kenosis*, and even more particularly when our *kenosis* involves the very real and horrific pain of devastating circumstances.

Now, you may be thinking that this concept of transformative effectiveness in our darkest place of suffering, in *kenosis*, is really out there. Pain is pain is pain, and it can be a nightmare, and it can seem to last forever, and it can have us gripped in a relentless and merciless grasp. It can issue from wounds which are so wide and deep and cruel that it seems they could never be healed in a lifetime. Pain can hold us in a headlock against a cold brick wall, and push us to anguished limits. Pain is very real, and very miserable, and sometimes that excruciating grip is beyond words.

Yet, can we hold another reality also in our other hand, so to speak? Can we hold the pain in one hand, and in the other *the reality that God is with us even in that darkest place* of *kenosis*? Our God is the God of the darkness of the crucifixion as well as the light-drenched resurrection. God enters into that dark place with us, and is with us even when we cannot perceive any trace of the divine. God is profoundly with us in our dark place, and God being with us also means God is in us and touching us with healing and transforming touches, even if we cannot perceive God with us, or God's action within us. In fact, part of our *kenosis* may be precisely the challenge of perceiving God as absent from us.

Before you dismiss the concept of positive transformation coexisting with suffering, let me provide a little contemporary scientific support. Over the last twenty-five years there has been an increase in the study of a phenomenon known as posttraumatic growth, or positive psychological change resulting from the onset of highly challenging life circumstances or trauma, including serious and life-threatening illness or injury; physical, mental, or emotional abuse; war; and death of loved ones.[10] The evidence overwhelmingly supports that positive change can occur as a person reconstructs the way they view life, themselves, and how they fit into the

10. Tedeschi and Calhoun, "Posttraumatic Growth: Conceptual Foundations," 1–3.

world. "The psychological struggle with traumatic events can include un-ambiguously negative psychological effects, but it may paradoxically also include highly meaningful outcomes."[11] In fact, "we have been finding that reports of growth experiences in the aftermath of traumatic events far out-number reports of psychiatric disorders."[12] The distress experienced as a result of the trauma is not avoided, ignored or discounted in people who experience posttraumatic growth, but the suffering and positive growth ex-ist simultaneously,[13] and in some cases "posttraumatic growth may require that some distress persist to serve as a continuing impetus to posttraumatic growth."[14] The two realities—suffering and growth—necessarily coexist.

This paradoxical coexistence of distress and growth in some people can give rise to transformation:

> Posttraumatic growth describes the experience of individuals whose development, at least in some areas, has surpassed what was present before the struggle with crises occurred. The indi-vidual has not only survived, but has experienced changes that are viewed as important, and that go beyond what was the previous status quo. Posttraumatic growth is not simply a return to base-line—it is an experience of improvement that for some persons is deeply profound. . . . posttraumatic growth refers to a change in people that goes beyond an ability to resist and not be damaged by highly stressful circumstances; it involves a movement beyond pretrauma levels of adaption. *Posttraumatic growth, then, has a quality of transformation*, or a qualitative change in functioning, unlike the apparently similar concepts of resilience, sense of co-herence, optimism, and hardiness.[15]

The positive transformation has been found to relate generally to "change in relationships with others, change in the sense of self, and change in philosophy of life"[16] as observed in five domains: (1) a more profound

---

11. Calhoun and Tedeschi, "Foundations of Posttraumatic Growth: New Considerations," 93.

12. Tedeschi and Calhoun, "Posttraumatic Growth: Conceptual Foundations," 2.

13. Ibid., 2, 5.

14. Calhoun and Tedeschi, *Facilitating Posttraumatic Growth*, 22; see also Tedeschi and Calhoun, "Posttraumatic Growth: Conceptual Foundations," 12–13.

15. Tedeschi and Calhoun, "Posttraumatic Growth: Conceptual Foundations," 4 (italics added).

16. Calhoun, Lawrence G., and Richard G. Tedeschi, *Facilitating Posttraumatic Growth*, 11.

appreciation of life and a transformed sense of priorities; (2) warmer and more intimate relationships; (3) an increased sense of personal strength, (4) recognition of new possibilities or pathways in one's life; and (5) spiritual development.[17] Researchers report example after example of people who have undergone the darkness of a traumatic event and yet also have experienced the light of positive transformation. Spirituality has been shown to highly correlate with a person's experience of posttraumatic growth.[18]

The element of paradox here is not lost on the researchers themselves. "Each of the five domains of posttraumatic growth tends to have a paradoxical element to it that represents a special case of the general paradox of this field: *that out of loss there is gain*."[19] Furthermore, the researchers report that the paradox is also apparent to the trauma survivors themselves: "[r]ecognition of these paradoxes engages trauma survivors in dialectical thinking that is similar to that described in literature on wisdom and integrative complexity."[20] The paradox itself provides fruitful ground for a new landscape of thought and being. A *New York Times* article sums up the unexpected positive effectiveness and paradox inherent in posttraumatic growth: "Paradoxically, many grow even as they suffer. The way we cope with trauma is far more complex than once thought, and the way it molds us is similarly complex. We bend, we break, we repair and rebuild, and often we grow, changing for the better in ways we never would have if we had not suffered."[21]

Do some of the themes underlying these findings remind you of Paul's expression of the paradox of the cross? Two realities coexist, one painful and one of transformative growth. Paradox predominately characterizes the experience: gain comes from loss. There is an underlying effectiveness even in the midst of distress. Additionally, in relation to Paul's Christ pattern, we might trace elements of not only *kenosis* in the traumatic event and resulting distress, but *enosis* in the growth experienced in warmer and more intimate relationships, and even the beginnings of *theosis* as humans reach for the divine in a developing spirituality. In one study, as an example

---

17. Tedeschi and Calhoun, "Posttraumatic Growth Inventory."

18. O'Rourke, et al., "Measuring Post-traumatic Changes."

19. Tedeschi and Calhoun, "Posttraumatic Growth: Conceptual Foundations," 6 (italics added).

20. Tedeschi and Calhoun, "Posttraumatic Growth: Conceptual Foundations," 6 (internal citations omitted; citing two studies: Baltes, Staudinger, Maercker, & Smith, 1995; and Porter & Suedfeld, 1981).

21. Rendon, "Post-Traumatic Stress's Surprisingly Positive Flip Side."

of the fifth domain of developing spirituality, the researchers simply cite the words of one of their subjects:

> You think about getting through something like that and it's down-right impossible to even conceive of how you ever could. But that's the beauty of the thing . . . it's gonna have to be said because I believe that God got me through it. Five or six years ago I didn't have these beliefs. And I don't know what I would do without Him now.[22]

God is profoundly with us, even when we find ourselves in a crucible of pain with no initial awareness of God; and where God is, there is transformative effectiveness, even in the crucible.

When we are in the crucible, it is very hard to experience anything except for the pain. Yet, if we can direct ourselves—our thoughts and our actions—to something beyond that reality of pain, we may encounter the second reality of the presence of God with us in our dark place. Perhaps, as with my friend Carolyn, that reality is experienced simply in the fact that only God can be with us in the full measure of our suffering and pain. Perhaps that reality is found in the experience that somehow there remains a ground of our being despite the excruciating pain, held intact by what can only be the divine. Perhaps, at the limit of what we had perceived as our self, we encounter the Limitless.

When we begin to experience that second reality of God's presence and effectiveness with us even in our dark place, we also begin to make crucial connections between our *kenosis* and our moments of *enosis* and *theosis*. These two movements, of locating God even in our dark place, and of connecting our experience of darkness with our community and with our oneness with God, are critical. *Kenosis* by itself, viewed alone without the presence of God, and without its companions of *enosis* (our community and creation) and *theosis* (union with God), and without the hidden yet very real divine transformative effectiveness—*kenosis* cut off in this stark and isolated way describes a bleakly hopeless interior landscape.

But that constricted view is simply not the reality of our situation. God is with us even in our darkest place, as he has shown the many throughout the ages. *Kenosis* coexists with *enosis*, our community of loved ones and the creation all around us, and *theosis*, our union with God and all his good. Simply by making a connection among these three moments, *kenosis*, although still very painful, takes on a clearer place in our lives, and even

---

22. Tedeschi and Calhoun, "Posttraumatic Growth: Conceptual Foundations," 6.

new meaning. Moreover, the possibility of divine transformative effective-ness hidden in the moments of even *kenosis* ought to fill us with renewed courage that what appears to be only dark and futile may paradoxically be light-filled and fruitful—the paradox of the cross belongs to our experience also. *Kenosis* seen from this perspective is not all-engulfing and master of our lives, but given its correct and true place in our experience.

Many years ago I was praying in church before the tabernacle in a small side chapel of the church. I was on one side of the space. It was a cloudy day, and the skylight above yielded little light. Presently a woman walked into the other side of the space, and her uncontrollable sobbing penetrated my prayer. It seemed to me in my prayer that she was purple, a figure racked by intense pain, sadness, and hurt. It also seemed to me that God held me in that prayer, quelling my human instinct to stand, go to her and comfort her. He showed me what seemed to be her heart, a torn, hurting, painful wound, and seemed to invite my prayers into that space of unbearable pain. As I prayed into that terrible wound, I knew that only God could repair and heal what was before me, and yet somehow I was invited to participate through my prayer in God's touching, soothing, and healing. Almost miraculously to me, after several minutes the woman's sobbing slowed, quieted, and she heaved a great sigh. I heard her rise and leave. I asked God why he let me participate so tangibly in his comfort of the woman, but I did not receive the fullness of the answer that day.

Many years later, I was going through a period of very difficult spiri-tual darkness. It had come to an intolerable point for me, and I found my-self sobbing on the floor of my closet. My heart felt radically broken, the pain felt endless, no beginning and no end. The overwhelming pain was all that I could experience. As I drowned in my own tears and misery, an image and a knowing suddenly broke through my suffering. *I, too, was the purple woman.* My sobbing stopped as this powerful realization took hold. Like the purple woman all those years ago, even though I was immersed in the black darkness of my *kenosis*, I also had a real and present *enosis*, another person perhaps unknown to me, another community, in prayer for me at a moment when I could not pray for myself. Like the purple woman, although blindly groping in my *kenosis*, I also had a very real *theosis*, God present and in union with me in my dark place, actively touching, healing, and comforting me.

Simply realizing that I was the purple woman also, that my *enosis* and *theosis* were tangibly there and intact even though I did not have a felt experience of them (after all, I had been on the other side and knew it to be true), was enough to break the bleakness and hopelessness of my *kenosis*. In fact, much like the original purple woman, I sighed with relief, and even with joy. I had located God in my dark place, even though I could not perceive him. And, powerfully, I could in my role as the purple woman, have a new understanding of the unknown woman next to me, on the other side of the space, earnestly pouring out love and prayer for me. I could connect my *kenosis* with my *enosis*, the Body of Christ, my community that may be hidden across distance and even time but nevertheless stands with me, supporting me and petitioning for me. Further, I could connect my *kenosis* with the new desire to share this very moment of pain-encrusted beauty with my community, my *enosis*. In my role as the purple woman I had a deeper and more dynamic understanding of the God who loves me, and is constantly at work behind the scenes, beyond my awareness, to love, restore, heal, transform, and comfort me in my *kenosis*—a mysterious union of *theosis* even as I experience the suffering of *kenosis*. This union, though hidden, could be glimpsed in the sudden gift of that image of the purple woman, a ray of God's light penetrating and illuminating my darkness. When I could connect my pain with these two elements of community and divine union, what I was experiencing came into powerful and true perspective.

These two movements of locating God even in our dark place, and connecting our *kenosis* with our *enosis* and *theosis*, may not be easy at first. But you are not alone even in this effort, even as you feel the iron weight of ache and the sharp blisters of pain overmastering the constricted corridors of the little bird heart. Here your community, known and unknown to you, reaches out in prayer for you, even as now I write this prayer for you—may you experience the deep desire of God to be with *you*, and God's presence with *you*, even and especially in your darkest, loneliest, most painful place. Moreover, the divine comes to your assistance in asking the divine to come to your assistance. Just when you think you are indeed alone in a place so dark that even prayers will not form upon your lips, "the Spirit too comes to the aid of our weakness; for we do not know how to pray as we ought, but the Spirit itself intercedes with inexpressible groanings" (Rom 8:26). God is so close to us that the Holy Spirit whispers the unspoken prayers of our hearts; even the hidden beating and needing of our hearts are pressed to the loving ear of the divine. You are not alone even on the path to discovering that you are not alone.

When we stumble through the darkness of *kenosis*, sometimes we cannot perceive the connections between it and the lighter parts of our spiritual experience, our *enosis* and our *theosis*. Yet, the connections remain, and in fact provide clues as to the presence of a hidden divine effectiveness. Like Mother Teresa, sometimes we are able to uncover the hidden divine effectiveness simply by connecting the dots among the moments of *kenosis*, *enosis*, and *theosis*, as we found in the last chapter. Mother Teresa was able to do this almost immediately in the case of her exhausting walk through the streets of Calcutta; but it took many years for her to make this connection in the case of her spiritual darkness. Yet in both cases she discovered powerful connections between her present *kenosis* and the *enosis* of profound empathy with her community of the poorest of the poor, and the *theosis* of her ever-deepening union with Jesus in the poverty of his cross. As she teaches us through her example, if we find that the connections among our moments of *kenosis*, *enosis*, and *theosis* seem blurry, confusing, or refusing to yield clues as to some kind of hidden effectiveness, we should be patient. Remember the wisdom of the spiritual masters who have gone before us: God has mysterious ways of hiding effectiveness or even our own transformation from us precisely because knowledge of it would interfere with the effectiveness or transformation.

When we first set foot on this staircase of spiritual experience of ours, we are beginners, new to everything, and full of ourselves in ways we do not understand yet. As we start up the staircase we discover that we are not the independent and self-contained entities we thought we were. We are in deep and powerful relationship with the divine, and that informs every aspect of our being. As we climb the staircase, that relationship is the constant among all the moments of *kenosis*, *enosis*, and *theosis*. It is that relationship with the divine which touches, transforms, and brings us to a fuller realization of our true selves. Where there is relationship with the divine, in any moment of *kenosis*, *enosis*, or *theosis*, whether the presence of the divine is perceived by us or not, we can trust that divine transformative effectiveness is also present. So our staircase is simultaneously our ever-changing, moving and growing relationship with God, and our highly effective transformative upward path to God, which is also in and through God.

Immersed in the ever-changing colors of our staircase, we are touched and transformed by the divine touch which comes through all the colors of the rainbow of our fluctuating moments of *kenosis*, *enosis*, and *theosis*. Our climb fills us with a deepening awareness of our relationship with God. As

we ascend, we grow in our ability to perceive the heavenly realities in addition to those omnipresent earthly realities; we move from simply reacting to
the earthly circumstances around us to glimpsing the possibly paradoxical
heavenly reality also present. As we go higher, perhaps the heavenly interpretation of events becomes just as easy for us to perceive as the earthly. The
colors of our heavenly reality become more and more vivid, and then begin
to eclipse the earthly reality altogether. As we approach the highest parts of
the staircase, the heavenly reality becomes so vibrant for us that the earthly
reality pales into nothingness, and so we experience with Paul the leaving behind of things mere shadows (Col 2:17; Heb 8:5) for the heavenly reality, the
leaving behind of the partial for the full (1 Cor 13:9–12). Or as the hymn says,
"things of the earth will grow strangely dim"[23] as we focus more and more in-
tently on the divine reality. Although as earthly inhabitants we will continue
to experience that challenging divide between earthly and heavenly realities,
and the discrepancy between earthly and heavenly realities may continue to
give rise to trials, we may be encouraged increasingly by the vividness of our
glimpses of the heavenly reality to faithfully continue our ascent upward, to
look to what is unseen and eternal (2 Cor 4:17).

The very act of our concentrated gaze and intense awareness of God
as our central axis gives rise to transformation: "All of us, gazing with unveiled face on the glory of the Lord, are being transformed into the same
image from glory to glory, as from the Lord who is the Spirit" (2 Cor 3:18).
By training our eyes and heart on the Lord instead of the earthly, we may
become what we behold as we take on the "same attitude that is also yours
in Christ Jesus" (Phil 2:5), which is the Christ pattern Paul describes in Phil
2:6–11. Paul encouraged us to consciously shift our thoughts and minds
toward the pattern offered by Christ: "Do not conform yourself to this age
but be transformed by the renewal of your mind" (Rom 12:2). We, in our
hearts, minds, souls, and actions, began to express and confess the divine
image as patterned in and through Jesus Christ, precisely in and through
the effectiveness of God's transformative work in us as experienced in each
of those moments of *kenosis*, *enosis*, and *theosis*. In short, we are surely and
perceptibly changed toward likeness to Jesus Christ through each moment
of our walk up the spiral staircase of spiritual experience.

---

23. Lemmel, *Turn Your Eyes Upon Jesus*. The refrain of the song is: "Turn your eyes
upon Jesus,/ Look full in His wonderful face,/ And the things of earth will grow strangely
dim,/ In the light of His glory and grace."

But something else begins to happen when we have reached the higher parts of that staircase. For Paul there was a very close connection between personal transformation in and toward Jesus Christ, and communal transformation. Paul grasped that the transformation of individuals in and through Jesus Christ and his pattern (in and through moments of *kenosis, enosis,* and *theosis*) leads to the transformation of others, which leads to the transformation of still others. In fact, Paul intuitively knew that the proclamation and propagation of the gospel relied upon human beings and their expression of the Christ pattern. We can glimpse Paul's vision of how *mimesis* transmits the gospel in his first letter to the Thessalonians: "You know what sort of people we were [among] you for your sake. And you became imitators of us and of the Lord, receiving the word in great affliction, with joy from the holy Spirit, so that you became a model for all the believers in Macedonia and in Achaia" (1 Thess 1:5–7). Paul identifies himself as a person transformed by Christ toward likeness to Christ and his pattern. Now in turn, Paul provides an example of Christ and the Christ pattern to the Thessalonians. In response, the Thessalonians become imitators of Christ and the Christ pattern as expressed through Paul. As the Thessalonians become expressive of Christ, they in turn provide their own examples of the Christ pattern to the people of Macedonia and Achaia. Thus individual transformation carries its own divine effectiveness—it is effective to impart the Christ pattern, which powerfully impacts and transforms others in turn.

In fact, the divine operates to transform us not only for the sake of our own transformation, but for the sake of the transformation of others. Mysteriously, God not only reveals himself to us, but also makes us a part of his own self-communication to others. Let me explain what I mean by this by turning around our three moments of divine-human interaction—*kenosis, enosis,* and *theosis*—and considering them from the standpoint of the Trinitarian God.

As finite creatures we cannot apprehend the infinite God; yet God, wishing to make himself known to us, chose to communicate himself to us in love. In sending his son Jesus Christ into the world, God the Father uttered the Word in human tongue—the Word, Jesus Christ, which through the Holy Spirit resonates at a mysterious yet receptive depth in the human soul. Revelation as "summed up" by Jesus Christ[24] is love acting upon us, "penetrating even between soul and spirit, joints and marrow" (Heb 4:12),

24. Second Vatican Ecumenical Council, *Dei Verbum* 2.7.

piercing into a previously unknown region of soul. In the Christ event God comes to be with us, and the resulting encounter is at once undeniable and all but inexpressible. Once again we may detect the contours of our three moments of *kenosis*, *enosis*, and *theosis* of divine-human relationship in the divine outpouring, being-with, and transformative union with humans.

In divine *kenosis*, God pours himself out upon humanity,[25] emptying love upon us and opening himself to "divine vulnerability;"[26] moreover, "there is kenosis involved in God's committing his message to human words."[27] God communicates to us, and we are able to hear the message. Not only are we able to hear, but in fact we listen. We are created with an openness and ability to transcend self, for the very purpose of reception and recognition of revelation.[28] Yet, how we hear and whether we recognize and accept depends upon the individual hearer. "Were not our hearts burning within us?" (Luke 24:32) said the disciples who encountered yet did not recognize the risen Jesus Christ on the road to Emmaus. Something in our very being responds to the divine presence, whether we recognize and acknowledge it intellectually or not. Moreover, we respond at a deeply interior level—our hearts burn within us; we recognize the voice of the One who calls our name.[29] This mystical encounter takes place within the depths of the human soul, and the soul responds to and recognizes the One encountered.

It is in this moment of God-with-us, of *enosis*, that the soul encounters and experiences the fullness of divine love through revelation. God loves, God communicates this love beyond love; God is with us. This communication takes place at the most interior of levels, as "deep calls to deep" (Ps 42:8). Of course, the message of revelation is invitation, not requirement. It compels a response, but does not compel an affirmative one. Even the recognition of God does not compel an affirmative response in faith, for "[e]ven the demons believe . . . and tremble." (Jas 2:19). Yet a response of "yes" in faith triggers a transformation of the human soul. The responsive soul reorients toward God, just as a plant turns its leaves to the sun. The soul reaches back to God. The soul reciprocates in kind, with love and with the desire to be-with-God. By "be-with-God" I mean a desire to be in the

25. Phil 2:7; Fee, "New Testament and Kenosis Christology," 30.

26. Fretheim, *Suffering of God*, 78; see 79–148. Compare Kitamori, *Theology of the Pain of God*.

27. Brown, *Critical Meaning of the Bible*, 17.

28. Rahner, *Foundations of Christian Faith*, 29, 58.

29. John 10:4; 20:16; Isa 43:1.

presence of God, a longing for God, a joy taken in God for himself, and crucially, a consent to the operation of God upon oneself. In the same sense that Julian of Norwich suggested that we are "oned" or knitted together with one another and with God,[30] the soul seeks to be-with-God. The soul identifies the God of revelation as its source and completion, and out of responsive love entrusts herself to his hands for such integrating needlework.

In the culminating moment of *theosis*, God wraps the soul in a transformative embrace of love, an embrace effective to remake and change his beloved one into a new creation reflecting the divine (2 Cor 5:17). A soul truly responsive to revelation is transformed by the very message of revelation itself, Love[31] which invites the beloved "to share in the divine mystery of the life of the Trinity."[32] One cannot be touched by God and remain unchanged; in fact, the mystics suggest that the *purpose* of these touches is to change us and draw us closer to him.[33] It is only through such a transformation triggered by revelation that we may experience an ultimate unity with God, as we "come to share in the divine nature" (2 Pet 1:4). Yet the transformation instigated by revelation encountered is not simply for the sake of transformation alone. The total impact of revelation includes *theosis* and thus further transmission of the message; we are so loved that we are integrated into the plan of salvation as divinized instruments of God. We ourselves become the way that God chooses to communicate the divine pattern and message to our fellow brothers and sisters.

A metaphor borrowed from the mystics helps to paint a picture of how this works. Imagine a bride, deeply in love with her divine Bridegroom, yet so far from perfect that she cannot hope for union with the Perfect. She seeks her Beloved night and day, and longs for her Beloved. Yet it will take the help of God to bring her to a state more worthy of union with him. To this end, God takes her heart as his beloved target, and shoots a chosen arrow of Love, which is the Bridegroom himself. This chosen arrow, because it is the divine Bridegroom, has the transformative power to penetrate the bride's heart deeply, and transform her being toward the divine likeness of

---

30. Julian of Norwich, *A Book of Showings to the Anchoress Julian of Norwich*, 322. Julian suggests that we are in a great union of love with one another and Christ: "For God is in man and in God is all." Julian of Norwich, *Showings* (Paulist), 192; see also 191, 210.

31. "What, do you wish to know your Lord's meaning in this thing? Know it well, love was his meaning. Who reveals it to you? Love. What did he reveal to you? Love. Why does he reveal it to you? For love." Julian of Norwich, *Showings* (Paulist), 342.

32. John Paul II, *Fides et Ratio*, § 13.

33. See, for example, John of the Cross, *Spiritual Canticle*, 485.

her Bridegroom. As the bride is transformed, she herself becomes the new divinized arrow of her Bridegroom, able to stand in his place as an instrument of transformation of others.

I am describing the classic archery metaphor of mystics derived from scriptural text found in the Song of Songs, also known as the Song of Solomon. The Song of Songs has been interpreted as a metaphor for both the relationship between God and his people, and the relationship between the individual soul and God.[34] Origen, Gregory of Nyssa, Bernard of Clairvaux, Teresa of Avila, and John of the Cross are but a few of the many who have found transformative significance in the bride's wound of love in the Song of Songs ("I am wounded by love." Song 2:5).[35] Origen, Gregory of Nyssa and John of the Cross have each interpreted the wound as from an arrow which represents God as revealed in the Person of Jesus Christ:

> The bride praises the bowman for his good marksmanship because he hits her with his arrow. . . . The bridegroom's arrows have penetrated the depths of her heart. The archer of these arrows is love [1 Jn 4:8] who sends his own "chosen arrow" [Is 49:2], the only-begotten Son. . . . O beautiful wound and sweet blow by which life penetrates within![36]

As the bride encounters this arrow of revelation deep within her soul, life penetrates within. The result is complete transformation of the bride, so much so that she herself becomes like the arrow—Jesus Christ—who has penetrated her soul.[37]

---

34. Commentary in the NAB describes the Song of Songs as "the sublime portrayal and praise for the mutual love of the Lord and his people." *New American Bible*, 742. "In Christian tradition, the Song has been interpreted in terms of the union between Christ and the Church, and, particularly by St. Bernard, of the union between Christ and the individual soul." Ibid., 743. The first Christian writer to compose a commentary on the Song of Songs was Hippolytus of Rome. Origen, Athanasius, Gregory of Nyssa, Theodore of Mopsuestia, Theodoret of Cyrus, and Maximus Confessor followed. But Origen's *Commentary* was the masterwork from which others borrowed, finding profound meaning in the text of the Song regarding God's relationship with, and transformation of, the individual soul. Origen, *Song of Songs*, 6. Gregory of Nyssa's commentary has also been influential. Gregory of Nyssa, *Commentary on the Song of Songs*. Bernard of Clairvaux is well known for his commentary on the Song, and a complete translation of his *Sermons on the Song of Songs* is available from Cistercian Publications of Kalamazoo, Michigan, in four volumes. See also Teresa of Avila, *Meditations on the Song of Songs*; John of the Cross, *Spiritual Canticle*.

35. See also Song 5:7.

36. Gregory of Nyssa, *Commentary on the Song of Songs*, 103.

37. Ibid.

This archery metaphor may seem a little perplexing at first reading, but please remember it is simply an allegory, attempting to describe something divine and mysterious, an action of God taking place on a spiritual level. The God of the universe works growth, transformation, and restoration all around us in creation, silently and sometimes almost imperceptibly. The seed germinates, the rose blooms, the child takes first steps—the inner self also germinates, blooms, and walks according to that sometimes-hidden infusion of divine creative power and love. Our loving God is constantly at work within us; as Paul wrote to the Philippians, "God is the one who, for his good purpose, works in you both to desire and to work" (Phil 2:13). Think of our arrow here not as a weapon but as an instrument of transformation—Jesus himself—delivered powerfully and supernaturally, deep within the self or soul. Like the bride, we deeply desire and welcome both our Jesus and our ensuing transformation, even when our hearts ache with our "wound" of love and longing, because it brings us ever closer to the One we love in growing and deepening relationship and union.

Importantly, the transformation is not simply for the sake of our transformation alone. God not only penetrates the soul with the arrow of life, but then uses that transformed soul to penetrate the lives of others. Gregory of Nyssa asserts that the bride herself becomes the arrow, held in the hands of the archer (Song 2:6).[38] Therefore, "God is both the bridegroom and the archer. He treats the purified soul as a bride and as an arrow aimed at a good target."[39] In this sense the soul becomes *logophasic*, or the speech of the Word.[40] The bride ascends from the pupil to the teacher[41]—through his divine transformation of her, she in turn may act as an instrument to catalyze transformation in others.

I love this word *logophasic*, because it precisely states what our business is as Christians—we are to be the living speech of the Word, Jesus Christ. We are called to *express and confess Jesus Christ* and his pattern while we are here on earth. And because we are beloved and transformed instruments of God, our very expression and confession of Jesus Christ is

38. "Earlier we said that the bride was the target; she now sees herself as the arrow in the bowman's hands." Ibid.

39. Ibid.

40. Laird, *Gregory of Nyssa*, 155, 168–169. "Speech of the Word" cannot occur without the corresponding "breath" of the Holy Spirit. Downey, *Understanding Christian Spirituality*, 38.

41. The Bride's heart has become "a honeycomb full of every kind of instruction." Laird, *Gregory of Nyssa*, 167.

effective to inspire expression and confession of Jesus Christ in others. Paul knew that the power of being no longer Paul but Christ in Paul was that he could be a living expression of the Christ pattern, an example which spoke to others about how to become the same, "no longer I, but Christ lives in me" (Gal 2:20); they in turn could do the same for others, and so on, passing living examples of the Christ pattern all the way down to you and me. That truly is our singular task—to faithfully and authentically speak the Word of God with our very being, to express and confess Jesus Christ in and through our lives.

This archery metaphor helps us to envision the circular model of revelation which we considered above. The model begins with God shooting an arrow of love at the soul. The soul is penetrated by the arrow, which transforms and divinizes the soul, effectively shaping the soul into a new arrow, which in turn is shot for the purpose of God's self-communication to, and transformation of, another soul—and so on, and so on. God's continual pouring out of self upon us (*kenosis*), being with us (*enosis*), and the resulting transformation of us (*theosis*) represents the continual impact and unfolding of revelation on both individual and community levels. Christian love is the imitation and *logophasic* expression of Jesus Christ (Phil 2:1–5), which issues forth on the community level as scripture, church, and our collective tradition of interpretation and transmission of the gospel. On an individual level, the soul transformed by the mystery of revelation desires to shout it out, to become the speech of Christ. Acknowledgment of the mystery of revelation necessitates that Christians "open themselves to it, proclaim it in their faith, celebrate it in the community, intensify their involvement in it, and make it the central factor in the important decisions of their lives."[42] This communication is precisely the furtherance of God's revelatory self-communication through the instrumentality of humans, the continual unfolding of the impact of revelation under the influence of the Holy Spirit. With *logophasic* proclamation by scripture and church, as traced by and exhibited in our collective tradition, the impact of revelation reverberates and ripples continually outward. In the individual context, the *logophasic* communication not only impacts other individuals, but also continues to bring the individual soul back into intimate contact with the instigating mystery of revelation, which in turn continues to transform the individual, which also in turn continues to inspire *logophasic* communication, stoking flame into more energetic fire with each cycle.

42. Baum, *Man Becoming*, 66.

But what does it look like, all of this? How does it show up in human form? I would suggest that we see it daily in the simplest expressions of Christian love. Love from God pours out upon us in the very place where we stand, love which triggers something inexpressibly beautiful and blooming in our hearts, love which may then cascade from us into the hearts of others.

Jesus Christ asked Mother Teresa to come be his light in the slums of India: "My little one—come—come—carry Me into the holes of the poor.— Come be My light.—I cannot go alone—they don't know Me—so they don't want Me. You come—go amongst them, carry Me with you into them. . . . fear not—it is I in you, with you, for you."[43] This "spouse of Christ" through her vows as a Missionary of Charity thus became the light of Christ himself to the poorest of the poor. No longer Teresa, but Christ in Teresa, she had become the effective transformative instrument of the divine. Wherever she encountered the dark "holes of the poor," she lit lights as Christ himself asked and empowered her to do. In a speech given in 1981 in Australia, she described lighting one such light:

> Then I entered one of those little rooms. I call it a house but it's only one room, and inside the room everything. So I told the man living there, "Please allow me to make your bed, to wash your clothes, to clean your room." And he kept on saying, "I'm alright, I'm alright." And I said to him, "But you will be more alright if you allow me to do it." Then at the end he allowed me. He allowed me in such a way that, at the end, he pulled out from his pocket an old envelope, and one more envelope, and one more envelope. He started opening one after the other, and right inside there was a little photograph of his father and he gave me that to look at. I looked at the photo and I looked at him and I said, "You, you are so like your father." He was so overjoyed that I could see the resemblance of his father on his face. I blessed the picture and I gave it back to him, and again one envelope, second envelope, third envelope, and the photo went back again in the pocket near his heart. After I cleaned the room I found in the corner of the room a big lamp full of dirt and I said, "Don't you light this lamp, such a beautiful lamp. Don't you light it?" He replied "For whom? Months and months and months nobody has ever come to me. For whom will I light it?" So I said "Won't you light it if the Sisters come to you?" And he said "Yes." So the sisters started going to him for only about 5 to 10 minutes a day, but they started lighting

---

43. Mother Teresa, *Come Be My Light*, 98 (from a 1947 account by Mother Teresa of her encounter with Jesus).

that lamp. After some time he got into the habit of lighting. Slowly, slowly, slowly, the Sisters stopped going to him. But they used to go in the morning and see him. Then I forgot completely about that, and then after two years he sent word—"Tell Mother, my friend, the light she lit in my life is still burning."[44]

Mother Teresa entered, made a bed, cleaned a room, looked at a photograph, spoke words of kindness, dusted and lit a lamp—outward gestures reflecting her exterior *mimesis* of Jesus Christ. Her interior *mimesis* manifested in her gentle persistence, her caring attitude, her kind attention, encouragement, and Christian love. In and through this simple alphabet, the Word was spoken. The gospel message was transmitted through Mother Teresa's *logophasic* presence, words and actions. She was Christ's faithful arrow sent to a good target, a man who received her message and her light.

Just like a little child who knows where she is if she is with her mother, let us "accept the kingdom of God like a child" (Mark 10:15) and make our central focus and task to keep our eyes upon the One who is the central axis of our spiral staircase. God has promised and does promise to be with us, in all of the moments of our lives, and thus in all of our moments of *kenosis, enosis,* and *theosis.* For Paul, this unbroken and ever-deepening relationship with God involves keeping our gaze on the Lord and our eyes on the prize of God's upward calling in Christ Jesus, and is charged with supreme effectiveness to transform us and to accomplish God's "good purpose" in and through us (Phil 2:13). This divine effectiveness operates even in circumstances which appear dark on an earthly level, yet may impart light on a heavenly level. God's continual presence with us during all of our moments of *kenosis, enosis,* and *theosis* suggests that we experience divine transformative effectiveness in all of our moments, even when we cannot fathom what God is doing in our lives, or when the presence and touches of God are radically hidden from us. It is particularly difficult to perceive the transformative effectiveness of the divine when we are in our dark place; yet God is with us even and especially in our dark place. Paradoxically, we may experience gain from loss, light from darkness, growth even out of distress—all marks of the hidden yet effective divine presence with us in our dark place.

When we are in that dark place of extreme *kenosis,* two movements help to draw us out of that potentially isolated and desolate landscape—first,

44. Ibid., 339–340 (from Mother Teresa's speech, Corpus Christi College, Melbourne, October 8, 1981).

a realization that God is with us, located even in the dark bombed-out shell of our hearts; second, that this present darkness connects in a deeply profound way with our Christ-in-community and creation, our *enosis*, and our growing union with God, our *theosis*. These three moments belong together, overlap, are sometimes one and the same, and connect deeply with purpose and divine effectiveness.

As we progress along our journey upward on our spiral staircase of spiritual experience, we may notice a subtle shift in our perception, priorities and vision—the earthly "grows strangely dim" in comparison with the wellspring of love and joy at our core, our central axis God. We increasingly experience citizenship of the heavenly, rather than the influence of the earthly. Something else begins to happen also—as we encounter God's revelation to us, respond, and are transformed, we also become empowered to impart the same message by our very being and lives. Increasingly able to reflect and live out the Christ pattern as we are called in our own way, we become the "chosen arrow" of God to impact other good and beloved targets. As we walk our staircases of spiritual experience and become more aware of the presence of God, we also become equipped to bring the presence of God to others. Loved by and in love with the One who is with us even in our darkest places, how deeply we desire to carry him and his divine light into the dark holes of others.

Chapter 7

Fitted to the Bow

Paul's Joy

IN PERHAPS THE DARKEST moment of the twentieth century, during the height of Hitler's regime in Germany, and after several of his associates in an underground Christian organization resistant to the Nazis had been systematically killed, Dietrich Bonhoeffer prepared a last circular letter to his remaining colleagues on November 29, 1942.[1] Aware that these deaths were likely a harbinger of other deaths, including his own, Bonhoeffer grappled with the question of what stance and attitude this band of out-lawed Christian pastors shared in the face of these appalling circumstances, and what attitude they ought to share also with their underground flocks. Like St. Paul writing to the Philippians from the confines of a merciless and deathly prison hundreds of years before him, Bonhoeffer chose as his resounding theme apparently the most paradoxical and surprising message of all—joy.

> A sort of joy exists that knows nothing at all of the heart's pain, anguish, and dread; [such anguish] does not last; it can only numb a person for the moment. The joy of God has gone through the poverty of the manger and the agony of the cross; that is why it is invincible, irrefutable. It does not deny the anguish, when it is there, but finds God in the midst of it, in fact precisely there; it does not deny grave sin but finds forgiveness precisely in this way; it looks death straight in the eye, but it finds life precisely within it. What matters is this joy that has overcome.[2]

1. Bonhoeffer, *Conspiracy and Imprisonment*, 6–7, 377.
2. Ibid., 378.

Similar to Paul, Bonhoeffer spoke of living out of a true Christian joy, a joy which remained untouched by the grim earthly realities surrounding him and his compatriots. "Joy abides with God, and it comes down from God and embraces spirit, soul, and body; and where this joy has seized a person, there it spreads, there it carries one away, there it bursts open closed doors," he wrote.[3] His message rings clear: our Christian joy is of and from God, speaks of something invincible and far beyond our present experience, and points to our eternal citizenship in the city of joy. Like Paul before him, Bonhoeffer's message of joy was written in the face of imminent suffering and eventual death: he was seized by the Gestapo a few months after composing this letter, imprisoned for almost two years, put on trial for conspiring to assassinate Hitler, and was executed by hanging on April 9, 1945, less than a month before the German surrender.

As Bonhoeffer's response of Christian joy even in the ominous situation surrounding him attests, joy is not to be confused with what we think of as happiness. We can be happy that we got the job, that a friend is getting married, that we graduated, that we are not incurably sick. The ebb and flow of our lives produces encounters with people, experience of events, and developing consciousness which can give rise to a wide spectrum of emotional responses, including happiness. But Christian joy is something beyond this experience of earthly happiness, and in fact beyond all experience deriving strictly from the earthly. This joy in God and from God eclipses all, and can be present in all, from our worst moments to our best moments. This joy bursts forth in those moments when the heavenly intersects profoundly and unforgettably with our earthly experience. This joy has at its core the recognition that we are in real relationship with God, and that this divine-human relationship of love goes beyond the parameters of human limitations, life, and death.

Joy springs forth from a deep knowing of the profound truth that, as Paul said, "Love never fails" (1 Cor 13:8). This relationship of love we have with Love itself is what matters, is what nourishes us, is what transforms us, is what powers us, and *is always victorious*. Moreover, *nothing* can separate us from the love of Christ (Rom 8:35–39), and we prevail completely over all earthly challenges through him: "in all these things we conquer overwhelmingly through him who loved us" (Rom 8:37). This life we have with Love triumphs over all, including death: "'Death is swallowed up in victory. Where, O death, is your victory? Where, O death, is your sting?'. . . . thanks

3. Ibid., 377–378.

be to God who gives us the victory through our Lord Jesus Christ" (1 Cor 15:54–55, 57). This unfailing love and victory we have in and through Jesus Christ is cause for great joy, even and especially in a cruel first-century prison, even and especially staring down the barrel of Nazi Germany, even and especially in your dark place and in my dark place.

Paul not only experienced and expressed joy in Jesus Christ, but he also realized that joy was the consistent mark of the Christian, the sign of both inward and outward response to the person and promises of Christ. In fact, for Paul, the singular and powerful response to all we have said so far about our upward calling in Christ Jesus is joy and rejoicing: "Rejoice in the Lord always. I shall say it again: rejoice!" (Phil 4:4). For Paul, joy and rejoicing were the ultimate expression that the Christian had been de-centered by Jesus Christ, had put on the specially-crafted lenses of the paradox of the cross, and could perceive reliably the hidden heavenly perspective and choose it over the earthly perspective. It was the ultimate expression that the Christian could trust implicitly and completely in the divine effectiveness operating in and through all circumstances, bringing about the heavenly victory. And perhaps most importantly, it was the ultimate expression that the Christian was living out of the Christ pattern, in faithful inward and outward *mimesis*, and could bind herself intimately to Christ in all moments of *kenosis*, *enosis*, and *theosis*. For Paul, joy was the response of Christians to (1) their relationship with God and one another; (2) the divine effectiveness underlying everything and the assurance of divine victory; and (3) the fulfillment of their individual and collective purposes in and through God.

Before we go further into Paul's joy in Jesus Christ, let us take a moment to consider Paul's foundational understanding of the concept of joy. As we have noted before, Paul's thought was deeply imbued with Hebrew scripture, and scripture very often served as his point of departure as an apostle of Jesus Christ. At least some consideration of what meanings, significance and nuance attached to "joy" as it came down to Paul will assist us in exploration of his use of it.

In Hebrew scripture, "the experience and expression of joy are close to one another;"[4] that is, part of the inward experience of joy is the outward expression of joy. Because joy "has a cause and finds expression,"[5] joy as found in Hebrew scripture naturally links the internal experience with ex-

---

4. Conzelmann, "χαίρω, χαρά, συγχαίρω," 363.
5. Ibid.

ternal physical manifestations such as dancing, clapping, shouting, singing and other external expression.[6] Moreover, joy is directly connected with experience of community—joy "aims at sharing, especially as festal joy."[7] References to joy and rejoicing abound in Hebrew scripture, and the experience of joy always has a connection to God. Some key themes found in Hebrew scripture involving joy include: joy and delight in the Lord himself as well as his commandments and word; joy in the presence and companionship of the Lord; joy in the transformative effectiveness of the Lord; joy taken in victory won in and through the Lord, as well as salvation and safety in the Lord; joy in prophetic fulfillment; nuptial joy, parenthood, and prosperity as gifts of the Lord.

Paramount among all of these various expressions of joy is simply joy taken in the Lord and in relationship with the Lord: the joy of the soul is the Lord (Ps 4:8, 43:4, 149:2) and the presence of the Lord (Ps 16:11; 21:7). Closely related are joy in the Lord's law (Ps 1:2), decrees (Ps 119:14, 111), righteousness (Ps 67:5, 68:4), works (Ps 92:4), merciful love (Ps 90:14), comfort (Ps 94:19), wisdom (Wis 8:16; Sir 6:28), and word (Jer 15:16). In contrast, the withdrawal or absence of the Lord as reflected in waste or vanity results in the absence of joy or gloom (Isa 16:10, 24:10–11; Joel 1:12; Bar 2:23). Yet redemption and the vindicating return of the Lord reinstate joy, which in turn chases away the gloom and sorrow (Isa 35:10, 51:11).

A theme of joy in God's restoration and transformative effectiveness is abundantly present, particularly in Isaiah. The primary metaphor for this theme in Isaiah is a transformation by the Lord of waste and desert into fruitfulness and rich land; for example: "Yes, the Lord shall comfort Zion and have pity on all her ruins;/ Her deserts he shall make like Eden, her wasteland like the garden of the Lord;/ Joy and gladness shall be found in her, thanksgiving and the sound of song" (Isa 51:3). God constantly renews and restores the land, making it fruitful and fertile (Ps 65:10–14); the effect is that joy itself clothes creation: "the hills are robed in joy" (Ps 65:13). Isaiah 55:12 also reflects great rejoicing of creation amid the effectiveness of God's word to accomplish his purpose: "Mountains and hills shall break out in song before you,/ and all the trees of the countryside shall clap their hands."

This divine restoration extends to God's people also. Salvation is directly connected with joy: "With joy you will draw water from the fountain of salvation" (Isa 12:3; see also Isa 9:1–2; Isa 35:10; Ps 105:43). God's

6. Harvey, "Joy," 1000.

7. Conzelmann, "χαίρω, χαρά, συγχαίρω," 363.

action rescues and restores his people, cause for the greatest of joy: "Those whom the Lord has ransomed will return and enter Zion singing, crowned with everlasting joy;/ They will meet with joy and gladness, sorrow and mourning will flee" (Isa 51:11). The lowly and the poor have joy in the Lord (Isa 29:19). Joy in the Lord as a refuge and protector recurs thematically in Psalms (e.g., Ps 5:12). Joy is found also in the help of the Lord (Ps 13:6, 63:8). Joy is taken in both God's saving action and in God himself, who saves, protects and helps even those on the margins of society.

Closely associated with joy in God's saving action is joy in victory, especially an unlikely or seemingly impossible victory brought about by the Lord. Such a victory can be experienced in situations as intimate and personal as the conception of a child, as in the case of Hannah, who was barren but enabled to conceive Samuel by God (1 Sam 1:5, 20). Hannah worshiped God in her joy: "My heart exults in the Lord,/ my horn is exalted in my God./ I have swallowed up my enemies;/ I rejoice in my victory" (1 Sam 2:1). Or such a victory could be on the battlefield, literally or figuratively. In the case of an outnumbered Judah facing multiple enemies, God assured his people, "Do not fear or lose heart at the sight of this vast multitude, for the battle is not yours but God's" (2 Chr 20:15). Judah simply sent out the singers to praise God, while "the Lord laid an ambush" (2 Chr 20:22) against their enemies, and then they "celebrat[ed] the joyful victory the Lord had given them over their enemies" (2 Chr 20:27).

The prevalent theme of joy in victory over an oppressive enemy (Ps 20:6; 21:2; Zeph 3:15) is also closely connected with joy in prophetic fulfillment. In fact, expressions of joy in Psalms and Isaiah often culminate in prophetic and eschatological (also known as end time) fulfillment (e.g., Ps 14:7, 53:6, 126:2, 5; Isa 9:2, 12:6, 25:9, 51:3, 61:10, 65:17–19, 66:14);[8] and the joy is the greater because the victory is final and complete.[9] Joy is a consistently important part of praise and worship, by the people (Deut 16:15; Ps 27:6; 47:2, 6; 71:23, 98:6; 107:22), by creation itself (Ps 98:8), and by both together (Ps 98:4). Moreover, the act of rejoicing in the Lord itself functions as a source of strength: "Do not be saddened this day, for rejoicing in the Lord must be your strength" (Neh 8:10). Joy also flows from the gifts of God: a spouse (Prov 5:18; Sir 26:2), children (1 Sam 2:1; Prov 23:24–5), harvest (Isa 9:2), and wine (Ps 4:8; Sir 31:27–28).

---

8. Ibid.

9. Langis, "Joy: A Scriptural and Patristic Understanding," 49.

Finally, nuptial joy occurs in Hebrew scripture in the context of the joy experienced by the earthly bride and bridegroom, but also, and in fact primarily, in describing the relationship between God and his people. In Isaiah, human and divine joy may be reciprocal and even have a nuptial character; the soul may say, "my God is the joy of my soul" (61:10), and God may take Jerusalem as a bride: "For the Lord delights in you, and makes your land his spouse./ As a young man marries a virgin, your Builder shall marry you;/ And as a Bridegroom rejoices in his bride so shall your God rejoice in you" (Isa 62:4–5); similarly, "For he who has become your husband is your Maker" (Isa 54:5). The people of God, or alternatively the individual soul, are "precious in my eyes" and loved by the Lord (Isa 43:4).

In the Song of Songs, which inspired the archery metaphor we considered in the last chapter, the love relationship between the bride and the bridegroom is often interpreted as a metaphor for both the relationship between God and his people, and the relationship between the individual soul and God. Not surprisingly, the joy and delight in the Song flow from this intense and central relationship, and joy takes on a distinctively nuptial character. The day of marriage is "the day of the joy of his heart" (Song 3:11). The Song contains references to rejoicing (1:4), and to delight in the beloved (1:2; 4:10; 5:16; 7:7). In fact, the entire text overflows with the delight which both the bride and the bridegroom experience in one another. Image follows on image of nuptial delight, longing, belonging, and love. Of particular importance to our present topic is the way in which joy in the beloved is sustained even when partnered with longing during separation from the beloved (Song 5:6), and even in the suffering of the bride, whose pursuit of the absent bridegroom leads her to experience the wounding blows of the watchmen (Song 5:7–8).

So a substantial number of references to joy in Hebrew scripture disclose a clear pattern of joy in connection with experience of God and God's actions. The relationship between God and his people or the individual soul, the effective action of God upon or with his people or the individual soul (to save, to protect, to comfort, to guide, to transform, and to love), and the fulfillment of the promise to be with and save his people or the individual soul all give rise to joy. In further fulfillment of the relationship-based quality of this joy, the responsive souls tender this very joy back to Lord in joyful praise and worship. In this sense, joy could be understood as an internal and shared external manifestation of a living, breathing, intricate and continuing relationship with God—the giving and receiving of joy indicate and characterize a key part of God's relationship with his people.

With this influential tapestry of joy as expressed in Hebrew scripture in mind, let us now turn to Paul. Writing to the community at Philippi not only while held captive in a merciless prison, but also facing the grave possibility of execution, Paul confidently chooses joy as his shocking, soaring and paradoxical message. In his relatively short Letter to the Philippians, Paul uses variations of the Greek word *chara* (joy) sixteen times; the noun "joy" appears five times, and the verb "rejoice" is employed eleven times.[10] The pertinent verses are: Phil 1:4 ("praying always with joy"); 1:18 ("in that I rejoice. Indeed, I shall continue to rejoice"); 1:25 ("for your progress and joy in the faith"); 2:2 ("complete my joy"); 2:17 ("I rejoice and share my joy with all of you"); 2:18 ("you should also rejoice and share your joy with me"); 2:28 ("on seeing him, you may rejoice again"); 2:29 ("Welcome him . . . in all joy"); 3:1 ("my brothers, rejoice in the Lord"); 4:1 ("my brothers, whom I love and long for, my joy and crown"); 4:4 ("Rejoice in the Lord always. I say it again: rejoice!"); and 4:10 ("I rejoice greatly in the Lord"). Because of this extensive and consistent refrain of joy and rejoicing, the letter is known as "the letter of joy," and provides an excellent frame of reference for our consideration of what Paul meant by his encouragement to joy and rejoicing.

In each of these instances of Paul's use of joy, elements of relationship, divine effectiveness, and fulfillment may be detected, which resonates with joy as found in Hebrew scripture. However, Paul's use of joy not only resounds with the fullness of meaning as found in Hebrew scripture, but he takes it to even another radically joyful level, because he finds new and even more significant meaning in taking joy in God through his experience of the Lord Jesus Christ. Paul experiences joy in God in a new and expanded way: (1) in *relationship* with the divine, now not only God the Father, but also the Son, Jesus Christ, and the Spirit, and moreover in and through Christ as present in and through other Christians; (2) in the new and profound experience of God's *effectiveness* and victory even through the cross, and therefore through the most extreme, painful, hidden, humiliating, and deathly of circumstances; and (3) in a new understanding of God's completion and *fulfillment* of his people in and through the Christ event, which was also a fulfillment of prophecy found in scripture.

10. Cousar, *Philippians and Philemon*, 19.

Paul, ever the pastoral father of his communities, was powerfully moved to teach the Philippians how to respond to their present challenges and persecutions. Paul taught directly out of his own experience, and used himself and his circumstances, as well as his own inward and outward responses to instruct the Philippians. His ringing and repeated calls to joy in the letter serve as an instructional signpost: when Paul takes joy or rejoices, he means for us to not only understand the powerful and victorious reasons why he rejoices, but to share in his joy ourselves, and moreover to imitate his response of joy in our own lives and experiences. In short, Paul's joy is not just about Paul, but *his joy is precisely our real and present joy also*. Paul wants us to feel the intense and triumphant joy in our loving, transformative, and life-giving relationship with the Lord. Paul wants us to be jubilant in the fact that the Lord always effectively and victoriously accomplishes his purpose despite earthly appearances. Paul wants us to overflow with delight as we realize that we are brought to completion and fulfillment as we increasingly progress in our upward calling in Christ Jesus, and as we undertake and accomplish the purposes for which we were created, in and through the Lord.

Paul does not ignore or minimize the reality of pain, loss, and suffering which the world may present to the followers of Jesus, himself included. Rather, as we considered in our first two chapters, Paul stands in the gap between the earthly reality of the relentless and often cruel crush of the world, and the heavenly reality of God and the kingdom of God. Although Paul experiences the trial of the discrepancy between these two very real and often paradoxical experiences, he also experiences the joy of bringing his perception and grasp of the heavenly into his experience of the earthly. It is as if Paul, with a foot in both worlds, stands simultaneously in both trial and joy, because he stands in overcoming through Christ Jesus. Whatever we are experiencing in the earthly, it does not touch upon the heavenly reality and our ultimate victory over the earthly circumstance. Or, as Paul explains: "What will separate us from the love of Christ? Will anguish, or distress, or persecution, or famine, or nakedness, or peril, or the sword? . . . No, in all these things we conquer overwhelmingly through him who loved us" (Rom 8:35, 37). Although we may experience many types of painful and dark realities, we simultaneously have the joy of knowing they have no power to triumph over us; rather, we "conquer overwhelmingly" or in other translations, "overcome" or "prevail completely," or are "more than conquerors" in and through Christ. Therefore, even writing from prison facing the possibility of death, Paul confidently proclaims this joy that overcomes (Phil 1:18–20; 2:17–18). Trial may come from below to challenge us about our distance from the heavenly reality, but joy comes pouring down from above to sustain us in our fight; trial may be the break and divide between the earthly and the heavenly, but joy is the miraculous bridge which allows us to overcome that chasm. Joy springs from our hidden yet unmistakable connection with the divine, which empowers us to endure and prevail in any circumstance.

Paul, having experienced this himself, wanted to share this incredibly joyful truth with his communities not only because it provides joy, but because it provides a joy-filled touchstone for the Christian attitude and stance in life, particularly in the face of life's challenges. With this in mind, we can see that Paul's refrain of joy in the Letter to the Philippians functions as a crucial set of instructions to teach the community about how to perceive and handle events, both exteriorly and interiorly. Paul's many and varied expressions of joy provide example upon example to the Philippians about how to respond to their present challenging circumstances: specifically, how to take joy in Jesus Christ and his pattern, how to perceive the paradox of earthly and heavenly realities, how to sense the paradoxical divine effectiveness underlying events, how to detect and find joy in Jesus Christ in these things and in one another, how to uncover in their own hearts and minds the progressive and transformative impact of God, and how to steadfastly and peacefully live out of that transformation as a shining light to all—all cause for joy.

It is worth briefly noting that the varying contexts of Paul's expressions of joy serve also to point out the pervasive quality of true Christian joy. From the most interior of situations such as prayer, love, thought, feelings about suffering and death, and *mimesis* of the attitude of Jesus, to the most exterior elements such as events, outcomes, behaviors, and interactions with one another, Paul attaches joy and rejoicing to a wide spectrum of Christian life. Paul draws upon his own internal and external joy and rejoicing to teach internal and external joy and rejoicing, and encourage shared joy among Christians. Utilizing himself and others as examples in Philippians, Paul asserts the presence of Christian joy in many venues, for instance: in prayer (1:4); in finding evidence of God's effectiveness even in apparently negative external events (1:18); in fostering joy in the faith (1:25); in unified community expressive of the attitude of Christ (2:2); in being poured out after the pattern of Christ (2:17); in shared joy (2:17–18);

in one another and the body of Christ (2:28–29); in a growing and faithful Christian community (4:1); in the Lord (3:1, 4:4); in rejoicing in the Lord as the hallmark of a Christ-oriented interior landscape (4:4); and in shared concern and provision for one another (4:10). The overflow of Paul's joy into so many aspects of interior and exterior life signals not only his irrepressible joy in God and the desire to share this expansive joy with others, but also a desire to cultivate the same limitless Christian joy in his communities.

Although at first reading these expressions of joy may appear unconnected or superfluous, upon closer scrutiny we may detect the themes of joy in relationship, joy in divine effectiveness, and joy in fulfillment through Jesus Christ intersecting with each mention of joy and rejoicing in the letter. In fact, a methodical examination of the use of joy in Philippians uncovers a consistent network of these three themes.[11] Yet for our purposes a simple appraisal of Paul's joy in relationship, divine effectiveness, and fulfillment in and through Jesus Christ will serve to illustrate the foundation underlying Paul's crescendo of joy. Implicit in this joy also is Paul's joy in fostering and sharing the same joy with the Christian community. Paul by example and through the shorthand of joy teaches his beloved Philippians—and you and me today—to discover and take up the melodic refrain of joy in relationship, divine effectiveness, and fulfillment, regardless of the world's cacophony.

First and foremost, relationship with the triune God—particularly as revealed so vividly in and through the person of Jesus Christ—serves as the wellspring of joy for Paul. Paul's deep and intimate bond with Jesus Christ forms the basis for almost every aspect of the letter, and for that matter, of his very being. Paul's refrain in Phil 3:1, 4:4 and 4:10 of rejoicing in the Lord, and actually, all of his uses of joy in Philippians, resonate with his fundamental and life-changing joy in Jesus Christ. Paul draws deeply on Hebrew scripture to interpret his transformative experience of Jesus Christ. For Paul, the prophetic joy of Hebrew scripture has come to fulfillment in the event and person of Jesus Christ. In all the senses of joy found in Hebrew scripture, Paul experiences joy in Jesus Christ: in his presence (Phil 4:5), in his protection (4:7), in his empowerment (4:13), in his victory (1:19), in his peace (4:7), in his affection (1:8), and in his power to transform (2:13; 3:21); moreover, his joy is the greater because it is all in fulfillment of prophecy and promise, a joyful fact which Paul carefully propounded in his letters.[12]

11. Hogan, *Pauline Theology*, 131–166.

12. For example, Paul asserted fulfillment of the prophetic text of Isaiah on many

But in all these facets of joy, what remained for Paul the most powerful cause for joy was simply the Lord himself (4:4, 10). The Lord is Paul's life (1:21), strength (4:13), and ultimate goal (3:14), and joy in the Lord is his constant refrain. The depth, richness and power of Paul's relationship with the Lord cannot be overemphasized, and neither can his accompanying joy.

Paul's joy in relationship with the Lord also stems from his experience of Jesus Christ in and through his community in Jesus Christ—in this case the Philippians. Consider for example Paul's expression of joy in Phil 1:4: "praying always with joy in my every prayer for all of you." Paul's joy takes place in prayer, which is his conversation and communion with God; yet the joy is also intimately connected with his experience of "all of you"—the Philippians. In Phil 1:7, Paul avers to the Philippians that "I hold you in my heart." This signifies not simply an intimate connection between Paul and the Philippians, but because Paul's own identity is so intertwined with Jesus Christ ("no longer I, but Christ lives in me," Gal 2:20), it also points to intimate connection among Paul, the Philippians, and Jesus Christ ("how I long for all of you with the affection of Christ Jesus," Phil 1:8). Moreover, Paul's stated reason for this intimacy is "you who are all partners with me in grace, both in my imprisonment and in the defense and confirmation of the gospel" (Phil 1:7). So the Philippians too have felt and expressed a connection between themselves and Jesus Christ, and themselves and Paul. We see expressed, therefore, an intimate three-part bond among Paul, the Philippians, and God, a relationship giving rise to joy (2:28–29; 4:1). Elsewhere Paul uses the metaphor of the body of Christ to illustrate this intimate bond of relationship (e.g., 1 Cor 12:2–30). All parts of the body of Christ, united with Christ and one another in and through Christ, share in the joy of each part of the body (1 Cor 12:26). Paul's beloved Philippians are "my joy" (Phil 4:1) in and through Christ; so too are those in his community at Thessalonica (1 Thess 2:19–20), and undoubtedly all his communities in and through Christ.

For Paul, relationship with Jesus Christ bursts not only with divine and powerful love (Gal 2:20; Rom 8:35), but also with the loving and saving activity of transformation—the love and presence of Christ inherently gives rise to transformation. Paul identifies Christ the savior by his power to "change our lowly body to conform with his glorified body" and "bring all things into subjection to himself" (Phil 3:20–21). Similarly, in 2 Cor 3:18

---

levels in Romans, particularly with regard to his gospel and mission. Wagner, *Heralds of the Good News*, 353. Wagner explores powerful references to Isaiah in Rom 9:1–29; 9:30—10:21; 11 and 15.

Paul powerfully describes the transformative effect of the Lord: "All of us, gazing with unveiled face on the glory of the Lord, are being transformed into the same image from glory to glory, as from the Lord who is in the Spirit." Paul cannot contain his joy and rejoicing in the Lord in part because of this astoundingly joyful aspect of the relationship—the divine presence and touch necessarily and effectively transform, and moreover, this transformation causes continual growth in likeness toward the Lord. Paul's joy in Jesus is deeply connected with his experience of being transformed by, and reflecting the pattern of, Jesus Christ (Phil 3:7–14), even if expression of the Christ pattern involves suffering (2:17). Additionally, Paul expresses joy at the prospect of the Philippians also coming to express the pattern of Christ (2:2–5). The bond among Paul, the community, and Christ also points to a shared experience of joy in and through relationship with the transforming person of Jesus Christ.

We catch glimpses of joy in relationship with the Lord in the lives of many holy people throughout hundreds of years, and often their joy reflects the same qualities seen in Paul's joy. As an example, the Carmelite lay brother Lawrence of the Resurrection (1614–1691) took deep joy in the presence of God. Brother Lawrence credited his conversion to a sudden awareness of God's love for a winter tree. Seeing the tree bare and seemingly dead in mid-winter, Brother Lawrence was filled with a profound understanding of God's love and faithfulness to all his creation, for he knew that the tree would regain leaves and bear fruit.[13] This insight revealing God's loving presence with us at all times laid a bedrock foundation for Brother Lawrence, who made his life about constant relationship with God. He developed a simple method of aiming his heart and mind solely at constant loving awareness of the presence of God, and he experienced profound joy in the divine presence:

> I keep myself in his presence by simple attentiveness and a general loving awareness of God that I call 'actual presence of God' or better, a quiet and secret conversation of the soul with God that is lasting. This sometimes results in interior, and often exterior, contentment and joys so great that I have to perform childish acts, appearing more like folly than devotion, to control them and keep them from showing outwardly.[14]

---

13. Brother Lawrence of the Resurrection, *Practice of the Presence of God*, 89.

14. Ibid., 53.

Brother Lawrence took joy in God himself, and in God's presence and love, and also, like Paul, in the transformative quality of God's love—just as the barren tree would gain leaves and bear fruit, Brother Lawrence would after years of great effort acquire a graced, consistent awareness of the presence of God. Also like Paul, Brother Lawrence took joy in relationship with God even in his moments of suffering. According to his biographer, as he approached death "[i]t looked as if he never had a moment's discomfort even when his illness was the most painful. Joy appeared not only on his face but even in his manner of speaking, causing the friars who visited him to ask him if he really was in pain."[15]

St. Elizabeth of the Trinity (1880–1906), a Carmelite nun who died painfully of Addison's disease at age twenty-six, also found her joy, and her heaven, in relationship with God, explaining in a letter to a friend:

> [T]he Carmelite already lives as if in Heaven: "by *God alone*." The same One who will one day be her beatitude and will fully satisfy her in glory is already giving Himself to her. He never leaves her, He dwells within her soul; more than that, the two of them are *but one*. So she *hungers for silence* that she may always listen, penetrate ever deeper into His Infinite Being. She is identified with Him whom she loves, she finds Him everywhere; she sees Him shining through all things! Is this not Heaven on earth![16]

Elizabeth explained to her mother in a letter that the secret of her happiness despite her advancing illness was found in 1 Peter 1:8; in her words, "Because you *believe* you will be filled with an unshakable joy."[17] In another letter she confided to a friend that the words of Ephesians 1:24 inspired her: "'In my own flesh I fill up what is lacking in the passion of Christ for the sake of His body, which is the Church.' The apostle finds his happiness in this! The thought pursues me and I confess that I experience a profound inner joy in thinking that God has chosen to associate me in the passion of His Christ."[18] Elizabeth found her joy despite immense pain in her deep relationship with the indwelling Trinity, which she called her "Three," and in her increasing union with the suffering Christ.

We can see in the cases of Brother Lawrence of the Resurrection and St. Elizabeth of the Trinity that, like Paul, relationship with God powered

---

15. Ibid., 121.
16. Moorcroft, *He Is My Heaven*, 96.
17. Ibid., 119.
18. Ibid., 161.

their lives and became their joy. They also exemplify how joy so deeply rooted in divine relationship remains unshaken even in suffering. Yet how would joy in divine relationship look today, even and especially in the presence of pain?

Stephen Colbert, an American comedian and late-night television talk show host, has surprised more than one of his interviewers with his interpretation of joy. Despite the intense pain of losing his father and two of his brothers in an airplane crash when he was only ten years old and the subsequent years of grief and suffering, he expresses a deeply felt gratitude to God. As he explains it, "that impulse to be grateful wants an object. That object I call God. Now, that could be many things. I was raised in a Catholic tradition. I'll start there. That's my context for my existence, is that I am here to know God, love God, serve God, that we might be happy with each other in this world and with Him in the next [world.]"[19] His experience of the presence of God is expressed in the Pierre Teilhard de Chardin quote which he kept on a paper taped to his computer for many years: "Joy is the most infallible sign of the presence of God."[20] He credits his mother Lorna for instilling in him the attitude that the heavenly perspective outweighs the earthly experience: "even in those days of unremitting grief, she drew on her faith that the only way to not be swallowed by sorrow, to in fact recognize that our sorrow is inseparable from our joy, is to always understand our suffering, ourselves, in the light of eternity. What is this in the light of eternity?"[21]

Like Paul, Lorna Colbert remained in unbroken relationship with God even and especially in her pain. Like Paul, she chose to keep her eyes on the heavenly perspective, on God. Despite her harrowing earthly trial of losing her husband and sons, she stood in not simply sorrow, but also in overcoming through her faith, and joy met her—the joy of Paul, of Bonhoeffer, of Brother Lawrence, of Elizabeth of the Trinity—the joy that arises from, and points far beyond our present experience, beyond life and death, to God. Also like Paul, her example of this was a shining light to be followed by other members of the body of Christ, including her son Stephen. Today Stephen Colbert lives out of the same sense of gratitude and joy, and by living it provides this example to others also.

The second powerful source of Paul's joy is divine effectiveness, or God's supreme and infinite ability to accomplish his divine purpose despite

19. Lovell, "The Late, Great Stephen Colbert."
20. Strauss, "The Subversive Joy of Stephen Colbert."
21. Lovell, "The Late, Great Stephen Colbert."

or even through dark, humiliating, humble, painful or deathly circumstances. Although previously aware of the effectiveness of God as found in Hebrew scripture, Paul perceived a new and stunning depth of divine effectiveness through his grasp of the paradox of the cross of Jesus Christ. What to our earthly eyes and understanding is death, is paradoxically life—our earthly understanding is turned on its head and eclipsed by the heavenly reality. The same divine effectiveness underlying the cross also informs every aspect of our lives as Christians. Paul's refrain of joy in Philippians declares the joy of this hidden and paradoxical effectiveness no matter what the circumstance—how joyful to know and experience that, as he says elsewhere, "all things work for good for those who love God, who are called according to his purpose" (Rom 8:28). In Philippians, Paul's experience of joy in divine effectiveness also is marked by hiddenness and paradox, often manifested as an experience of two competing realities. Although faced with suffering and apparently defeating circumstances, Paul does not express disappointment or despair, but rather a refrain of joy. Paul perceives this hidden yet irrepressibly effective power in all circumstances, events, and relationships, and considers it a very high priority to teach his communities to perceive divine effectiveness and take joy in it.

Paul takes joy in recognizing himself and his own situation as persuasive evidence of divine effectiveness, and takes further joy in revealing to the Philippians the otherwise perhaps hidden and paradoxical effectiveness of his own ministry and imprisonment. Paul joyfully interprets the fact of his own imprisonment, a situation which should deter proclamation of the gospel and give rise to despondency, as effective to increase boldness of proclamation of the gospel (1:18); additionally, even those who preach Jesus Christ for selfish motives still function to proclaim Christ (1:15–18). Both of these facts which reveal God's effectiveness even through Paul's imprisonment are cause for joy: "And in that I rejoice" (1:18). Moreover, Paul "shall continue to rejoice" (1:18) because even his suffering and imprisonment "will result in deliverance for me" (Phil 1:19)—Paul is confident that, "with all boldness, now as always, Christ will be magnified in my body, whether by life or by death. For to me life is Christ, and death is gain" (Phil 1:20–21). Paul's message takes on additional depth because he speaks with the voice of the long-suffering Job: "this will result in deliverance for me" (Phil 1:19) is "an exact quotation of five Greek words from the LXX text [of Job 13:16] that mean 'This will turn out for my salvation.'"[22] Significantly,

22. Osiek, *Philippians, Philemon*, 41. The LXX, or the Septuagint, is an approximately

the preceding verse from Job is, "Slay me though he might, I will wait for him" (Job 13:15). Paul chooses Job's voice here not only "to affirm confidence in the favorable outcome of his afflictions"[23] but also to support and heighten the stunning and paradoxical fact of his rejoicing.

According to the earthly perspective, the looming specter of his imprisonment ending in death seems terrible—yet Paul rejects that perspective. He confidently (cf. Phil 1:6, 25, 3:3–4) chooses the heavenly perspective instead. His death would be, just as his life is, an example of divine effectiveness at work (Phil 1:20). And he cannot rejoice enough at this incredibly freeing and joyful truth. Paul not only takes the time to explain this to the Philippians, but he also exhorts them to join in his rejoicing. He teaches them by his own example to have confidence in, and take joy in, the paradoxical heavenly perspective, and to perceive God's effectiveness in every circumstance, no matter what the external appearance. Significantly, his lesson is a practical one. For like Paul, the Philippians also have been "granted, for the sake of Christ, not only to believe in him, but also to suffer for him" (Phil 1:29). Paul involves the Philippians with him through shared struggle (Phil 1:30) and shared joy—through the love of Jesus Christ which binds them all together, they will together choose and share the one response appropriate to the prospective yet sure effectiveness of God: joy.

Paul's multiple expressions of joy in the Philippians themselves also reflect his keen observation of God's effectiveness. Paul concludes that his intense labor and outpouring of time, self, energy, work, and teaching on the Philippians has not been futile (2:16), for the Philippians themselves "shine like lights in the world" (2:15). Paul perceives the Philippians also as living, breathing manifestations of the divine effectiveness of God—in fact, of the divine effectiveness of God through the efforts of Paul himself. The Philippians are proof of the paradox; they are proof that Paul's efforts, sufferings, and sacrifices have been, and continue to be, effective to transform through the grace of God. They are the result of his "fruitful labor" (Phil 1:22)—labor which was not in vain (2:16) but yielded great transformation. For the sake of this already-effective result, Paul will "continue in the service of all of you for your progress and joy in the faith" (Phil 1:25). In Paul's eyes, the Philippians themselves are "my joy and my crown" (Phil 4:1)—his joy in them is highly associated with his victory through and in them; they

---

2nd century BC translation of the Hebrew Bible into Koine Greek, which was utilized by Paul.

23. Hays, *Echoes of Scripture*, 22.

are the mark and evidence of God's effectiveness to transform through the person and work of Paul.[24]

We can see that Paul's rejoicing stems directly from his observation that divine effectiveness is precisely at work in moments of self-emptying and seeming defeat; just as Jesus Christ's victory came through the cross, Paul's victory comes through Jesus Christ even in moments of self-sacrifice and seeming defeat, such as his imprisonment in defense of the gospel. We observe this powerfully in Paul's most concentrated and intense use of joy in Philippians (Phil 2:17–18): "But, even if I am poured out as a libation upon the sacrificial service of your faith, I rejoice and share my joy with all of you. In the same way you also should rejoice and share your joy with me."[25] In the context of the most dire of circumstances, not only does Paul rejoice, but shares his joy outwardly with the Philippians; moreover, he calls on them to rejoice and share their joy with him in fullness and reciprocity of joy. The Philippians were just most vividly reminded in Phil 2:6–11 of the sacrificial and perfect emptying of Christ, which resulted in exaltation. Just as the emptying of Christ in verse 2:7 conferred a salvific benefit on humanity, Paul's "pouring out" of self (2:17) will not be in vain but also will be effective to benefit others. Paul's imprisonment and possible execution, following after the pattern of Jesus Christ, will result not in death, but life; not in foolishness, but wisdom; not in weakness, but power; not in loss, but gain; not in vanity, but perfect divine effectiveness—cause for great joy.

By attaching this soaring joy to God's ultimate effectiveness even in the worst of situations, Paul accomplishes his teaching purpose through becoming, like the cross of Christ, a paradoxical and impossibly joyful sign that interrupts an earthly interpretation of events. It is precisely Paul's joy that reveals his steadfast grasp on the heavenly perspective, and communicates his utter confidence in God's effectiveness to render a somehow positive outcome even in the most negative circumstances. He is the joyful proof of the supreme effectiveness of the cross of Christ—Paul's suffering in the service of Jesus Christ will turn out for his deliverance, and moreover, through the spread of the gospel (Phil 1:12), for deliverance of many. Paul's joy profoundly reveals this hidden and paradoxical effectiveness—a

24. See also 1 Thess 2:19–20.

25. Paul also closely connects joy and suffering in 2 Cor 7:4: "I have great confidence in you, I have great pride in you; I am filled with encouragement, I am overflowing with joy all the more because of all our affliction." See also 2 Cor 8:2: "for in a severe test of affliction, the abundance of their joy and their profound poverty overflowed in a wealth of generosity on their part."

profound effectiveness which today we can recognize all the more given the benefit of knowing the actual and vast impact of Paul and his work.

Our contemporary Stephen Colbert also expresses a paradoxical experience of the effectiveness of God even in terrible circumstances. He explained to an interviewer that, "Boy, did I have a bomb when I was 10. That was quite an explosion. And I learned to love it. So that's why. Maybe, I don't know. That might be why you don't see me as someone angry and working out my demons onstage. It's that I love the thing that I most wish had not happened."[26] Asked by his flabbergasted interviewer to help him understand this better, Colbert immediately cited a letter written by J.R.R. Tolkien in response to a priest who had written questioning him regarding the treatment of death in his novels not as punishment for original sin but as a gift.

> "Tolkien says, in a letter back, 'What punishments of God are not gifts?'" Colbert knocked his knuckles on the table. "'What punishments of God are not gifts?'" he said again. His eyes were filled with tears. "So it would be ungrateful not to take *everything* with gratitude. It doesn't mean you want it. I can hold both of these ideas in my head."[27]

Colbert was thirty-five years old before he could "really feel the truth"[28] of this paradox. Somehow he came to feel grateful for the gift even as he still felt the awfulness of the loss. Perhaps it is this very paradox of gain even in loss which gave rise to the attitude of gratitude and joy in his daily life. His interviewer, obviously deeply impacted by Colbert's words, wrote: "The next thing he said I wrote on a slip of paper in his office and have carried it with me since. It's our choice, whether to hate something in our lives, or to love every moment of them, even the parts that bring us pain."[29]

One author finds that this remarkable ability of Colbert to "not only accept what had happened but actually to rejoice in it" is also an example of "the slow but sure unfolding of the divine plan"[30] involving a chain of people going through difficult, emptying experiences and passing the fruit of them to others. Bishop Robert Barron traces the insight of Tolkien embraced by Colbert back to Father Francis Morgan and then to John Henry Newman. Like Colbert, Tolkien lost his father as a child, when he was

26. Lovell, "The Late, Great Stephen Colbert."
27. Ibid.
28. Ibid.
29. Ibid.
30. Barron, "Unfolding the Divine Plan," 13.

just three years old in 1896. His mother Mabel afterward chose to live in Birmingham, England with him and his younger brother to be closer to her family. However, when Mabel decided to become a Catholic and raise her two sons in the faith, her family essentially abandoned her. She turned to the priests of the Birmingham Oratory for help, and they provided financial and spiritual care for her and her sons. When Mabel died in 1904, Father Francis Morgan, a priest of the oratory, became the guardian of Tolkien and his brother.[31] This kindly man acted as a father to the two boys, and greatly influenced Tolkien in matters spiritual and otherwise.

Barron speculates that Morgan "taught the young Tolkien, who had endured more trials than any child ought to endure, that 'all of God's punishments are gifts'"[32]—that sufferings could contain hidden gifts of God. Barron further asserts that Morgan himself received this insight from the founder of the oratory, John Henry Newman, who suffered "dark night experiences" at the time he established the Birmingham Oratory in 1848. At that time Newman, a new Catholic convert, was "excoriated as a traitor by the Anglican establishment and looked upon with suspicion by Catholics."[33] Yet out of this "dark night" there came fruit: the successful establishment of the oratory, and the insight of God's effectiveness even in the midst of suffering. This notion of God's gifting even through painful circumstances was absorbed by Father Morgan, who in his own self-emptying choice of providing fatherly care and financial assistance for two orphan boys could pass on this teaching to Tolkien, who in turn through his letter inspired the young grief-stricken Colbert. We can perceive in this chain of time, events, and people that God is effective despite dark circumstances even in passing the very message of divine effectiveness in and through dark circumstances—an enduring message of overcoming and joy.

The third foundational element of Paul's joy is his sense of fulfillment of purpose in and through Jesus Christ, on individual and collective levels of humanity. Paul experienced a deep sense of fulfillment of the purpose of his own life in and through Jesus Christ. In his Letter to the Galatians, Paul explains that God "from my mother's womb had set me apart and called me through his grace, was pleased to reveal his Son to me, so that I might proclaim him to the Gentiles" (Gal 1:15–16). He thus associates his very existence with his mission and purpose of proclamation of Jesus Christ.

31. Birmingham Oratory, "Tolkein and the Oratory."
32. Barron, "Unfolding the Divine Plan," 13.
33. Ibid.

Moreover, Paul read not only the Christ event as the fulfillment of Hebrew scripture, but very likely considered his own life and his mission to the Gentiles to be part of the fulfillment of prophetic scripture.[34] In Philippians, Paul portrays his fulfillment in and through Jesus Christ as an intimate, complex and dynamic experience. In his autobiographical account, we see Paul radically transformed in and through Jesus, conformed to his pattern, and sharing in his life and sufferings. Paul's desire to "be found in him" (Phil 3:9), "to know him" (3:10), "to possess it [perfection or fulfillment]" (3:12), and to single-mindedly pursue "the prize of God's upward calling, in Christ Jesus" (3:14) indicates that the shape and means of his fulfillment is Jesus Christ. He envisioned the same fulfillment for all in and through God's upward calling in Jesus Christ and his pattern.

Paul describes a curious tension in his experience of fulfillment in and through Jesus Christ. While he "has been taken possession of by Christ Jesus" (3:12; "possession" here meaning to enter into close relationship with), he has not similarly attained possession of Christ: "Brothers, I for my part do not consider myself to have taken possession" (3:13), although the fact that Jesus Christ possesses him gives him cause for hope that he will attain to possession of Christ (3:12).[35] Paul directly associates this notion of possession of, or entering into close relationship with, Jesus Christ with being brought to perfection, completion, or fulfillment (3:12). The Greek word at root here is *telos*, which has been variously translated as maturity, perfection, completion, fulfillment, goal, or end; but none of these translations evokes the dynamic sense of the word, which captures simultaneously both the sense of unfolding toward fulfillment and the sense of reaching a purpose or goal.[36] So there is an important element of *unfolding fulfillment of purpose* in this word, and a simple example communicates this elusive element: a book which is being read is in a state of *telos*; a book sitting on a shelf is not.[37] The meaning of *telos* thus intertwines with action which fulfills the purpose for which something was created.

Part of Paul's joy in Jesus Christ was this sense of the unfolding fulfillment of his life's purpose and existence in and through Jesus Christ.

34. Wagner, *Heralds of the Good News*, 353.

35. Hansen suggests interpreting the verb in terms of relationship: "A plausible meaning of this verb in this context is 'to enter into close relationship, receive, make one's own, apprehend/comprehend.'" Hansen, *Letter to the Philippians*, 250.

36. Delling, "τέλος, τελέω, ἐπιτελέω," 54.

37. I am indebted to Rev. J. Patrick Mullen of St. John's Seminary, Camarillo, California for sharing this example.

Moreover, part of Paul's joy in the Philippians was that he also sensed the same unfolding fulfillment of purpose in and through Jesus Christ happening in the Philippians: "I am confident of this, that the one who began a good work in you will continue to complete it until the day of Christ Jesus" (Phil 1:6). The Greek verb used in this verse, translated "to complete," is also part of the *telos* word group. Paul had a definite and joyful sense that God's purpose in and through his Son, Jesus Christ, was the unfolding fulfillment, completion or restoration of his people, through their upward calling in Jesus Christ.

With regard to his own personal experience of unfolding fulfillment in and through Jesus Christ, Paul's expression is marked by contradiction. In the same sense that Paul simultaneously "has been taken possession of by Christ Jesus" (3:12) yet does not possess Jesus (3:13), he says that he is not perfect or perfectly mature ("It is not that I have already taken hold of it or have already attained perfect maturity" (3:12) and yet almost in the next breath he says the opposite, "Let us, then, who are 'perfectly mature' adopt this attitude" (3:15). Scholars have puzzled over this inconsistency and its meaning. Gerald Hawthorne finds the second use ironic, rejecting the theory that Paul uses the words "in two different senses within such a short span of words, and thus there is no reason to translate one 'perfect' and the other 'mature.'"[38] Bonnie Thurston and Judith Ryan question whether the remark in verse 3:15 might be ironic, but settle on the interpretation that "those who are working *toward* perfection" should think as Paul thinks.[39] Charles Cousar rejects the notion that Paul employs irony here, noting that "nowhere else does he use *teleios* ironically, as well as the fact that he uses the term for himself."[40] Carolyn Osiek finds a resolution to the tension in "different nuances of the same word group."[41] Karl Barth, Markus Bockmuehl, and G. Walter Hansen arrive perhaps closest to the mark by finding that Paul's point is paradoxical: Christian perfection lies precisely in the attitude that one is not perfected.[42]

---

38. Hawthorne, *Philippians*, 156.

39. Thurston, et al., *Philippians and Philemon*, 131.

40. Cousar, *Philippians and Philemon*, 77.

41. Osiek, *Philippians, Philemon*, 99.

42. Bockmuehl, *Epistle to the Philippians*, 226; Barth, *Epistle to the Philippians*, 111; Hansen, *Letter to the Philippians*, 258. This notion also resonates with the thought of very many classic spiritual theologians, who stress humility as the only path to perfection. See, e.g., Teresa of Avila, "While we are on this earth nothing is more important to us than humility." Teresa of Avila, *Interior Castle* (Kavanaugh), 292.

Certainly Paul's use is paradoxical. Yet this paradox points to much more than what Christian perfection is—it points to the very experience of it. Paul's rich expression of the paradox of Christian life was not academic; he lived it out on a daily basis. "We are treated as deceivers and yet are truthful; as unrecognized and yet acknowledged; as dying and behold we live; as chastised and yet not put to death; as sorrowful yet always rejoicing; as poor yet enriching many; as having nothing and yet possessing all things" (2 Cor 6:8–10). Paul's perception of two competing and paradoxical realities, one stemming from an earthly perspective and the other flowing from a heavenly perspective, extended to his experience of two realities regarding his fulfillment in Jesus Christ. On the one hand, Paul fights the fight of his life—he presses on despite all obstacles toward his purpose and fulfillment in and through Jesus Christ. But on the other hand, Paul is already profoundly experiencing a sense of unfolding fulfillment of purpose in and through Jesus Christ, of himself, of his communities, and of humanity. He is in the transformative and fulfilling embrace of Jesus Christ even as he still struggles to endure the fight and the race to arrive at his ultimate fulfillment and goal, the prize of God's upward calling in Christ Jesus.

Paul experiences joy in both of these senses of fulfillment. The bride in the Song of Songs takes deep delight in the presence of the Beloved, in everything about him ("he is all delight," Song 5:16; also 1:16; 2:3; 5:10–16), in his love for her (Song 1:2), and in mutual belonging to one another (Song 2:16). The deep love in her heart (he is "he who my heart loves," Song 1:7; 3:1) is expressed in an outpouring of words which ring with delight in him. Her delight in the Bridegroom is not diminished by separation or incompleteness of union; the bride continues to take delight in him even though she longs for him, pursues him, and suffers in the pursuit (Song 5:6–8). So, too, Paul takes joy in Jesus Christ both in being possessed by him and in the pursuit to take possession of him. Paul's joy in Jesus Christ stems from his experience that Jesus Christ is the one who completes and fulfills creation which is incomplete and unfulfilled without him. Love by its very nature requires the other, and in fact cannot be brought to completion without the other. Love is brought to fulfillment when those who love one another love, in moments of shared longing for one another when apart, and in moments of completeness when together, in both the present moment and in future moments of deepening relationship.

In a similar sense that a book fulfills the purpose for which it was created only with a reader, Paul finds his fulfillment only in and through

Jesus Christ, and the purpose for which he was created is fulfilled only in and through Jesus Christ. It is precisely in moments of experience of such fulfillment that Paul expresses joy in the Letter to the Philippians. As Paul interprets events and his own experience through the lens of Jesus Christ, for himself, the Philippians, and indeed the entire body of Christ, he cannot help his refrain of joy in the Lord. As he proclaims the Lord Jesus Christ in his actions, his words, and his very being and even his body (Phil 1:20; Gal 6:17), he takes joy in the way it conforms, unites, and fulfills him and his purpose in Jesus Christ. Moreover, Paul takes joy in seeing the Philippians similarly brought toward fulfillment through Jesus Christ, and the promise of further spread of the gospel through the Philippians, and then through their converts, all for the sake of, and through, Jesus Christ. They are becoming and doing what they were made by God to become and to do, and this is cause for joy which strains beyond self to God.

Thérèse of Lisieux also spoke of joy in the context of fulfillment of her purpose in Jesus Christ. She had a mighty desire deep within to serve God, in many different roles: "I feel the *vocation* of the WARRIOR, THE PRIEST, THE APOSTLE, THE DOCTOR, THE MARTYR."[43] Even as Thérèse felt frustration that she could not live out these particular vocations, she had the sudden realization through reading chapters 12 and 13 of Paul's first letter to the Corinthians that "love comprised all vocations, that love was everything, that it embraced all times and places. . . . in a word, that it was eternal! Then in the excess of my delirious joy, I cried out: O Jesus, my Love. . . . my *vocation*, at last I have found it. . . . MY VOCATION IS LOVE!"[44] Thérèse experienced great joy in the discovery of her vocation, her purpose in and through and for Jesus Christ. Yet in the lines that follow she also expresses the paradoxical sense of this fulfillment very like that of Paul himself. She has no doubts about her purpose or its origin: "it is You, O my God, who has given me this place; in the heart of the Church, my Mother, I shall be *Love*. Thus I shall be everything, and thus my dream will be realized."[45] Yet she also is cognizant of the obstacles which confront her in the fulfillment of her vocation, because she sees herself as a little bird without the means of accomplishing such a lofty goal: "Why do You not reserve these great aspirations for great souls, for the *Eagles* that soar in

43. Thérèse of Lisieux, *Story of a Soul* (Clarke), 192.

44. Ibid., 194 (some all-capitalizations omitted).

45. Ibid.

the heights?"[46] The eventual fruit of this paradoxical experience was also paradoxical; it was precisely Thérèse's "little way" of showing love to God and others through ordinary acts that elevated her to sainthood and the rare status of Doctor of the Church. The little bird needed to be exactly the little bird, in order to be simultaneously the eagle.

Can you enter into this paradoxical experience of fulfillment also? What does it feel like to simultaneously feel the completing embrace of Jesus, sensing the warm, alive, transformative and fulfilling presence wrapping around us, while at the same time knowing that we are still on our journey, on the sometimes challenging spiral staircase of our upward calling in Christ Jesus? Paul wanted us to experience the glow of joy in both of these senses of fulfillment. In the present, we already are being touched and transformed, and being brought toward fulfillment through Jesus Christ, even as we are still on the way, progressively climbing our staircase of God's upward calling in Christ Jesus.

In the Letter to the Philippians, the joy expressed by Paul and urged on the Philippians is powerfully and intimately connected with present experience. The question may be asked, however, whether the *cause* of that joy arises from present experience or anticipation of future experience. On the one hand, the letter contains numerous eschatological (end time) references (e.g., Phil 1:6, 10; 2:16; 3:21) and the content of the entire letter in one way or another points dramatically and continuously to "the prize of God's upward calling in Christ Jesus" (3:14), and the emphasis on suffering for the sake of the gospel indicates orientation toward a future goal. Yet on the other hand, as we have considered, Paul experiences genuine and overwhelming joy arising from *proof and experience of the presence of God in present events and people.* An occurrence which discloses the deep bond of relationship in and through Jesus Christ, or divine effectiveness surely at work, or transformation in growing likeness to Jesus Christ, hinting at completion, fulfillment—all these experiences belong to the present moment and in themselves fill Paul with joy. After all, Paul does not say "our citizenship will be in heaven," but he instead says, "our citizenship is in heaven" (Phil 3:20). In the present moment, we are citizens of heaven, and as such we may experience the presence of God, which is the first and foremost cause of joy, both in Hebrew scripture and in Paul's Letter to the Philippians.

Like Paul, we also may experience joy in the here and now even as we also are "straining forward to what lies ahead" (3:14), which is Joy itself.

46. Ibid., 197.

Our joy is centered in our living and breathing relationship with the Lord and one another in and through the Lord, our deep sense of divine effectiveness in any given situation, because we use our specially-crafted lens of the cross to perceive the true reality of things, and our unfolding fulfillment of purpose in and through Jesus Christ. Of course, each of these three elements of Paul's joy, and our joy, intertwine together—the transformative relationship with Jesus Christ and one another merges into the supreme effectiveness of the Lord to accomplish his purposes, which merges into the fulfillment of the very purpose of our lives in and through the Lord. The three flow into one joyful experience of the divine for Paul, and for us. As we walk our spiral staircase of spiritual experience, we have access to all these sources of joy, because they radiate from our central axis, God.

So my fellow little birds, imagine yourself once again on your beautiful and radiant spiral staircase—brilliant with shades of the bullet blue of your *kenosis*, the rosebud embrace of *enosis*, and the golden crown of *theosis*, all threading through you yourself and your staircase in imitation or *mimesis* of the One we love, Jesus Christ. The entirety of the staircase is held and supported lovingly by the central axis, which is a stunning bolt of pure light, beginning somewhere infinitely above, or perhaps having no beginning at all, being Infinity itself. This shaft of Light provides more than love and strength and light and the way, it provides life and the presence of our God with us—and therefore joy, abundant joy. So when we stretch our hand to this our central axis, or lay our cheek upon it in tearful distress, or rest upon it in exhaustion, or embrace it in hope, we catch a glimpse of the silvery moonlight of our own reflection, bathed in the pure light of Love and the joy which always accompanies. No matter where we are on this staircase, in blackest muddy holes, busy rabbit warrens, or brilliant mountaintops, we must hold fast to our center and support, the Light of the world (John 8:12). As we follow the sweeping way step by step, the colors of our landscape swirl and change, yet the Light remains. We must keep our fingers trailing in the rays of "his wonderful light" (1 Pet 2:9), always connected to the One who is with us.

Yes, our central axis and our One true source of joy is present and always at hand for us, in all our moments of *kenosis*, *enosis*, and *theosis*. Jesus encouraged us to draw deeply upon him in our living expression of him, in a mutual remaining in one another: "Remain in me, as I remain in you" (John 15:4). The pattern which Jesus set out for us is his own living pattern, and it is in our *mimesis* of Jesus in all our moments of *kenosis*, *enosis*, and *theosis* that we remain in him. Just as the vine sustains, powers, and informs the branches, the branches draw life, reflect and reach out from their source, bearing much fruit. Jesus, the Word, specifically desired that "you remain in me and my words remain in you" (John 15:7), an invitation to live out the speech of the Word in our *mimesis*, to express the pattern of Christ in and through our very being. Jesus himself connected this intimate living out of him, his words and his pattern with his own and our joy: "I have told you this so that my joy might be in you and your joy might be complete" (John 15:11). By remaining in him, his words and his pattern, and by allowing him to remain in us in and through his presence, words and his pattern, we become the joy of Jesus, and our own joy is made complete.

Paul experienced this, and shared his joy and his own particular expression of the words and pattern of Jesus with us, even as he encouraged us in finding our own individual expression of the same trustworthy Word and pattern, in all its moments of *kenosis*, *enosis*, and *theosis*. In the Letter to the Philippians, Paul expresses joy in the context of each of these moments. Paul took joy in his emptying and suffering, his *kenosis*, after the pattern of Christ: "even if I am poured out as a libation upon the sacrificial service of your faith, I rejoice and share my joy with all of you" (Phil 2:17). He took joy in the *kenosis* of others as they imitated the pattern of Christ, such as Epaphroditus: "Welcome him then in the Lord with all joy . . . because for the sake of the work of Christ he came close to death, risking his life" (Phil 2:29–30). Paul took joy in his *enosis*, his Christ-in-community, after the pattern of Christ on several levels. He saw his own work with them as fostering joy: "we work together for your joy" (2 Cor 1:24); "I shall remain and continue in the service of all of you for your progress and joy in the faith" (Phil 1:25). He took joy in the *enosis* of seeing this work blossoming in the communities, "your obedience [to the gospel] is known to all, so that I rejoice over you" (Rom 16:19; see also 2 Cor 7:16); as well as joy in *enosis* reflected in concern and care for one another (Phil 4:10; 2 Cor 8:2). Paul's greatest joy in his *enosis* is undoubtedly simply the communities themselves; they are "my joy and my crown" (Phil 4:1). Finally, Paul took joy in his transformative divine union, his *theosis*, which he viewed as a dynamic and progressive deepening of union, expression and confession of Jesus Christ. In Philippians, Paul's intense experience of union with Jesus Christ powers and shapes his being (e.g., Phil 3:7–12). He rejoices in the expectation that even in prison under threat of execution, "now as always, Christ will be magnified in my body, whether by life or by death" (Phil 1:20). He is so intertwined with the transforming Christ that he is "no longer I, but Christ lives in me" (Gal 2:20). Paul takes joy in the Lord, who empowers (Phil 4:13), transforms (2 Cor 3:18; Phil 3:21), clothes (Gal 3:27), and makes us a "new creation" (2 Cor 5:17). Paul's joy in *theosis* extends to other Christians who may also be transformed in union with Christ; his joy will be complete as the Philippians themselves are united among themselves in Christ and as they themselves are transformed and completed in Christ (Phil 1:6; 2:2–11; 3:21).

Yet even as we tease apart Paul's joy in these three moments of *kenosis*, *enosis*, and *theosis*, Paul himself is there to remind us that these three moments necessarily commingle for us just as they did for Jesus Christ. The exaltation of Jesus occurred precisely through his self-emptying for the sake of humanity (Phil 2:6–11). Paul experiences this melding of the three moments similarly—for example, "even if I am poured out as a libation upon the sacrificial service of your faith, I rejoice and share my joy with all of you" (Phil 2:17). We can see that Paul connects and conflates his "pouring out" of self (*kenosis*) directly with "sacrificial service" of the faith of his Christ-in-community (*enosis*), all in expression of, and in transformative union with Jesus (*theosis*) in his suffering for the sake of others. We can identify these three discrete moments even as they slide and completely fuse together. It is no coincidence that this confluence of the three moments results in Paul's most concentrated use of joy in Philippians (four expressions of joy in two verses, 2:17–18). In fact, the way Paul sees it, the joy is the greater in any situation for a Christian if it involves all three moments which merge together into an emptying of self (*kenosis*) in favor of another (*enosis*) which reveals transformative union with Jesus (*theosis*). He rejoices and shares his joy when these three moments connect together in a unity of perfect *mimesis*, and encourages his communities to do the same: rejoice and share their joy with him and one another (Phil 2:17–18). Through his letters, Paul also reaches down to us, encouraging us to take joy in his *mimesis* of Jesus Christ, the *mimesis* of others, and our own individual rendering of the pattern of Jesus Christ, even and especially at the intersections of painful self-emptying, connection with community, and divinized expression and confession of Christ.

If you start looking for these intersections in your life, you will find them. These three fused moments of divine-human interaction lie beneath unforgettable major moments, and also beneath the smaller, fleeting ones that may escape our notice if we are not attentive.

My son was born on a Good Friday in the afternoon. It was a planned caesarian-section birth. After I was prepped for surgery I was led to a narrow operating table, not much wider than the width of my body. After I was on the table, a nurse secured each of my arms on rests that were extended perpendicular to the table. Yes, weirdly I was on a cross-shaped table, and my mind went immediately to the sacrifice of Good Friday. All of the work, discomfort, pains, and heaviness of the pregnancy were coming to an end, but not without a final *kenosis*. The doctors cut my abdomen open, cut again through muscle tissue, moved organs out, cut again, and again. The umbilical cord was wrapped around my son's neck and there were some anxious moments as the doctors worked. Finally my son was born—I heard him, and then I saw him. He was beautiful, perfect, and he looked right at me. Love and joy flooded my heart, and tears poured down my face. The *kenosis* of the birth combined with the *enosis* of meeting my son for the first time with my husband, combined with the *theosis* of God's presence and union, and in the miracle of his creation of a life through my body—in this intersection, I was filled with joy.

But we need not look to something as major as a birth to find the intersection of an emptying of self (*kenosis*) in favor of another (*enosis*) which reveals transformative union with Jesus (*theosis*) which gives rise to joy. You can find that intersection in daily, ordinary life, and that is precisely what Paul expects us to do. In my own life I am surprised by these intersections even in very simple moments—our *kenosis* can be an outpouring of love in minor but heartfelt ways, like Mother Teresa's hug for Eileen. As an example, these days my son is a teenager and an avid soccer player, and he enjoys teaching a weekly soccer class at a local Catholic Charities community center for under-served children between six and ten years old. A few months ago when I accompanied him, a little girl had both of her shoelaces untied so I asked her if I could tie them for her. She said yes. At that time I happened to have a cast on my right foot so kneeling down was more laborious and painful than I expected (and was probably very comical too). After I tied her shoelaces, she looked at me with her big brown eyes, smiled brightly, and said, "Thank you!" In that moment I felt filled with joy—as if she were Jesus letting me love him through her, or as if I were Jesus and she was letting me love her through him. At the intersection of my slight but sincere *kenosis*, the connection of *enosis*, and the experience of *theosis* was joy. I think that she may have felt it also, because every time I go to the soccer class, she asks me to tie her shoelaces.

Perhaps ironically, even in moments overshadowed by sadness or pain we may sometimes detect this intersection of *kenosis, enosis,* and *theosis* giving rise to that joy which stands in overcoming. When my father was hours away from death, and I was sitting beside him on his bed, he roused himself from sleep and said to me, "I think I am almost through it." I broke down in tears of grief, and he held me in a hug I will never forget—he was comforting me for the loss of himself. It was a terrible, grief-stricken moment yet at the same time there was something other-worldly about him saying he was "almost through it," as if he were simply stepping out of a tunnel of blackness into somewhere better and brighter, and something other-worldly also about his peaceful hug, strangely both dying and comforting me regarding his dying. Although it took me years to understand, I experienced joy from above even in this terrible trial. Those moments were intersections of *kenosis, enosis,* and *theosis,* and perhaps more importantly, moments that pointed to something beyond the natural and death, to something that could not be touched by death or loss or pain. In those moments, we stood in overcoming through Christ and his pattern, and a solemn joy in the Lord was our strength.

As we increasingly become able to put involvement with sacrifice, suffering, and loss—our *kenosis*—in its proper place, as just one moment in our imitation of Christ which also includes, and connects with, our *enosis* and *theosis,* we are correspondingly able to grasp the hidden effectiveness of our experience, and draw from the joy of Christ with growing intensity and completeness. Paul gave us his own example of taking joy in blended elements of relationship, divine effectiveness, and fulfillment as they occur in moments of *kenosis, enosis,* and *theosis,* whether occurring separately or melded as one experience. We do not have to look far to discover other examples of joy and rejoicing in *mimesis.* St. Francis of Assisi reportedly instructed Brother Leo: "if we endure all those evils and insults and blows with joy and patience, reflecting that we must accept and bear the sufferings of the Blessed Christ patiently for love of Him, oh, Brother Leo, write: that is perfect joy!"[47] Dietrich Bonhoeffer wrote, "Only Jesus Christ, who bids us follow him, knows where the path will lead. But we know that it will be a path full of mercy beyond measure. Discipleship is joy."[48] Mother Teresa imparted to a friend, "Let the joy of the Lord be your strength.—For He alone is the way worth following,

---

47. Brown, *Little Flowers of Saint Francis,* 60.

48. Bonhoeffer, *Discipleship,* 40.

the light worth lighting,—the life worth living,—and the love worth loving."[49]
As soon as we put on Christ and began to consciously live out of his pattern,
we begin to learn how to connect our sacrifices and sufferings with the body
of Christ and with our increasing union with Christ. These connections put
the dark places of our lives into life-giving relationship with others and our
God, and remind us that we can take joy in our relationship with God, our
confidence in God's effectiveness, and our faith in God's fulfillment of promises, prophecy, and persons.

Paul marks out his joy as beacons for us, for his journey is our journey,
and his map of the upward calling in Christ Jesus is our map also. To survey
Paul's joy—and our corresponding joy—along this transformative path, let
us return to our archery metaphor of the last chapter. Paul takes deep joy in
being loved and transformed by Christ, the arrow which has hit a good target. Paul himself becomes an arrow of Christ through intimate relationship,
at a cost which is paradoxically all gain, and which will be used for God's effective purpose. Paul becomes the arrow because he has become "speech of
the Word"—that is, he has expressed Jesus Christ by his life and in his very
being, in all his moments of *kenosis, enosis,* and *theosis.* In becoming such
an arrow which will be used for God's good purpose in the transformation
of others, Paul has been fitted to the bow of God; he has come to know,
and take joy in, his purpose. In the Philippians and the other communities
which he fostered, Paul could perceive God's effective execution of purpose
in and through Paul—the arrow had hit the mark. In all these ways, in
intermingling elements of relationship, divine effectiveness, and fulfillment
of purpose, Paul took and shared profound joy, and encouraged us to the
very same joy. Let us rejoice also, then, in being fitted to the bow of God.

This joy which comes from above, this joy which stands in overcoming through Christ Jesus, is also the joy which marks the way along our
spiral staircase of spiritual experience, our upward calling in and through
Christ Jesus. As we know by now, this joy draws from the well of salvation,
a deep, transformative and fulfilling connection with God. This joy means
you have been de-centered by Jesus Christ, and have taken up his gift of the
cross as the lens through which you live. This joy is not of earthly concerns,
but pours down from above as we draw the heavenly into our earthly trials,
and we become proof of the hidden paradox of the cross, a sign which con-
tradicts the world. This joy stands in overcoming through Jesus Christ, with
utter confidence in divine effectiveness no matter how the circumstances

49. Mother Teresa, *Come Be My Light,* 264 (citations omitted).

appear. This joy knows it walks in and through the power of the living God, supported and nurtured as it makes its way through the moments of the pattern of Jesus himself—the painful darkness of *kenosis*, the ruddy glow of community in *enosis*, and the staggering gold of *theosis*. This joy leaps as we recognize this priceless pattern weaving within us and our lives, a singular pattern visible to others, a tapestry of *mimesis* all our own. This joy delights as it becomes fulfilled in its purpose of its upward calling in Christ Jesus, and as Jesus the great magnet draws it upward, this magnetized and divinized metal filing may draw others up besides.

You and I may wonder how such a magnificent, beautiful, and joyous pattern may be embroidered in and through the very being and life of a little bird with a heart bigger than her wings are able. Yet let us look through our specially-crafted lens of the cross, for according to Paul, our weakness and smallness are not a hindrance, but paradoxically, an advantage: "for when I am weak, then I am strong" (2 Cor 12:10). Thérèse of Lisieux knew that this joy was for the taking even for the smallest bird, who could see her world through such eyes of faith:

> At times the little bird's heart is assailed by the storm, and it seems it should believe in the existence of no other thing except the clouds surrounding it; this is the moment of *perfect joy* for the *poor little weak creature*. And what joy it experiences when remaining there just the same! and gazing at the Invisible Light which remains hidden from its faith![50]

This little bird gazes through the lens of the cross, paradoxically gazing at what is hidden and invisible. She perceives and holds the two realities of the heavenly and the earthly, and holds one in each hand. And like Jesus, like Paul, like Francis, like Mother Teresa, like Dietrich Bonhoeffer, she chooses the heavenly as her focus and guide. Therefore she remains "just the same"—choosing to live out of the heavenly perspective, regardless of the storm. This is the joy of the little bird.

The joy of the little bird is stirred precisely by the heavy dark clouds, because they give her the opportunity to be a sign in the world that the Invisible Light is present although hidden. She takes joy in perceiving the Invisible Light with her even when hidden behind those thunderclouds— she locates God with her even in her dark place. Even though she is very small, she can do a very big thing in very ordinary circumstances—by her gaze she reveals the Light to those who look only to the darkness of the

50. Thérèse of Lisieux, *Story of a Soul* (Clarke), 198.

storm. In this simple gaze, she empties herself of desire for something visible (*kenosis*), is a sign to others of the Invisible (*enosis*), and reflects her transformative unity with, and expression of, Jesus Christ (*theosis*), who also gazed at the hidden Father from the cross. Just as Mother Teresa lit a lamp and spoke the Word through this simple alphabet, the uninterrupted gaze of the little bird warbles the clear and effective notes of the infinite Word, chirped and trilled in her own humble yet delightful birdsong.

The little bird knows that the One upon whom she fixes her eyes is all—just as a child knows she is not lost if she is with her mother, the little bird knows it is not *where* she is that matters, but *Who* is with her, remaining by her side as her central axis, her strength, her love, and her Invisible Light. She can perceive the true state of things even when it remains hidden from her earthly sight. Even as she feels the cloudy trial of the distance between her earthly perch and the heavenly heights of her Light, the little bird is filled with the joy which stands in overcoming through Jesus Christ, bridging the gap and empowering her to keep her steady gaze and sing her song. Although perhaps not a sharp-taloned and fierce eagle screaming in the sky, she is a mighty warrior in her heart and mind. She fights the good fight with weapons which "are not of flesh but are enormously powerful," and she takes "every thought captive in obedience to Christ" (2 Cor 10:4, 5). In her interior and exterior *mimesis*, she voices her own completely individual expression of the shape of Jesus Christ, in all her moments of *kenosis*, *enosis*, and *theosis*, in shades of muck, leaf, and sky. Like Paul, she has the strength for everything through the Light who empowers her, as she winds her kaleidoscopic way up the spiral staircase of her spiritual experience. Like Paul, the little bird single-mindedly and victoriously beats her wings toward the goal, the prize of God's upward calling in Christ Jesus.

Conclusion

I Live, No Longer I

WHEN I WAS NINE years old, I asked my mother, "Why am I me?" I probably would not even remember that I asked this, except for the fact that I got a lump in my throat when I said it, and that my mother and my father could not answer the question. The question I was really asking at that time was: why out of all the people in the world do I happen to be me?

I have come to realize that this is part of the question we ought to be asking ourselves as we grow in our relationship with God. Each of us is a completely original creation, with our utterly unique gifts and hidden potentialities. Part of life is unwrapping this gift, and discovering not only who we are, and why we are, but ultimately who we are in Christ, and why we are—our purpose—in Christ. I live this rich and beautiful life given to me, yet no longer I—the greatest "I" I can be is the "we" of no longer me but Christ in me. And that I live, no longer I but Christ in me also tells me a lot about why I am, and why I am me, in my particular time, place, and person, just as you are also in your particular time, place, and person. We are all part of this living, moving, breathing Body of Christ, each with our own particular expression and confession of Christ, each with our own place and purpose, yet also in intimate connection and unity with the whole.

Our God loves to work through the ordinary, the unexpected, the small, the weak, the youngest, the outcast, the least. Scripture reveals again and again this preference for choosing the ordinary to reveal the extraordinary, the pouring of the divine into clear and humble human containers so that the glory of God may shine through without cloud. Paul said, "we hold this treasure in earthen vessels, that the surpassing power may be of God and not from us" (2 Cor 4:7). When you are thinking about why you are you, consider that part of why we are ourselves is to let all of God's glory shine through our simultaneously radically individual yet completely surrendered prism.

Do not be distracted or defeated by what you perceive as your ordinariness, your hiddenness, or your weaknesses. God delights in being with us and fulfilling his vision of us, wherever God finds us. When the angel of the Lord came to Gideon, he greeted him by saying, "The Lord is with you, mighty warrior." (Judg 6:12, NIV).[1] Gideon, baffled that the angel would address him this way and send him to lead Israel, objects that his "clan is the weakest" and that he is "the least in my family" (Judg 6:15, NIV). Yet despite, or perhaps because of, this weakness, he is indeed the one chosen as the mighty warrior. This is the pattern we see even more profoundly in the coming of Christ—God empties in order to come to, and into, us—whoever we may be, in whatever circumstance we find ourselves. If we are weak, then, according to Paul, that weakness is precisely our strength: "I will rather boast most gladly of my weaknesses, in order that the power of Christ may dwell with me. . . . for when I am weak, then I am strong" (2 Cor 12:9–10). Through Jesus, God is not only with us, but in us—in our humanity, in our weakness—and with and in us in such a powerful and transformative way that it redefines self and life.

In the same way that Thérèse of Lisieux was paradoxically both the little bird and the mighty eagle, we also are asked to look at ourselves, both who we are and who we might become, through the lens of the cross of Jesus. That lens is the key to discerning what is true and of value, including our own identity and path. Even as you hold in one hand the reality of yourself, all your gifts and limitations, all your positive and negative circumstances, and your sufferings and joys, in the exercise of your faith you also hold in your other hand that heavenly perspective, the reality of what all that means through the paradox of the cross, in the light of the sun which may be hidden but nevertheless still shines. You may experience the trial of earthly reality, but you know where to look to find the joy of heavenly reality pouring down on you also.

As the great magnet of Christ swoops down and catches hold of us, we are filled with his magnetizing power, which reorients and empowers us, and enables us to confess and express him through our very being. We slowly discover that each and every moment of our lives is charged with relationship with God—the divine is profoundly with us, in the darkness of *kenosis*, in the community of *enosis*, and in the union of *theosis*. These

---

1. NIV quotations utilize *The Holy Bible, New International Version*.

moments transform us, and may even transform others through us. When we can connect these moments together, we break the darkness of *kenosis*. We are not alone, but part of a vibrant community known or unknown to us in our *enosis*; we are not alone, but loved by God who is always present and drawing us into an ever-deepening transformative union with him, a *theosis* even in our experience of *kenosis*.

It is in walking through the vivid, ever-changing colors of your staircase of spiritual experience that you both live and find that you are no longer you, but Christ in you. As the divine expands in you through all these moments of relationship with God, as you move through life experiences and allow God to work in you through all your moments of *kenosis*, *enosis*, and *theosis*, transformation happens. Your "I" shifts in perceptible and imperceptible ways. Your focus begins to settle on God through all; your movements echo and reflect this. As you grow in your expression and confession of Christ, you may find also that you are living out the joyful fulfillment of your divine purpose: in being both your wonderfully made (Ps 138:14) individual self, and simultaneously no longer you but Christ in you, you discover why you are you.

We, each and every one of us, are made in the image and likeness of God (Gen 1:26). As we come to engage more deeply with what that might mean, and who we are in and through Christ, we grow and transform ever further toward the One we seek. Perhaps our path lies in hiddenness, perhaps it is cloaked in weakness and humility, or perhaps crucified; yet through the cross our way is also ultimately vital, triumphant, whole, powerful, and victorious. It may take some time for a little bird to find her "who" and "why" in Christ, to learn that her heart, her wings, and her song are mighty weapons. It may take practice runs, falls, mistakes, crashes and near-misses to rise higher. It may take great courage and persistence to take on the predators and the daily threats and burdens. But her seemingly humble appearance disguises the true and powerful reality revealed by the lens of the cross. She is a mighty and powerful eagle, an eagle built for everything God has in store for her. I hear the harmonies which God will make of her notes; I see the heights which God will make of her flights. I perceive the delight that God takes in making his small one an overcomer, a warrior, a victor, a sign of God's glory.

Paul experienced this electrifying intersection of the divine coming into him—into his humanity and life—and making him something greater than simply Paul. Over the centuries, he is calling out to us today to open ourselves to the same invitation: to live, no longer you, but Christ in you.

Bibliography

Adam, A.K.M. "Walk This Way: Repetition, Difference, and the Imitation of Christ." *Interpretation* 55 no. 1 (January 2001) 19–33.

Athanasius. "De Incarnatione." In *Contra Gentes and De Incarnatione*, edited by Robert W. Thomson. Oxford Early Christian Texts. Oxford: Oxford University Press, 1971.

Backherms, Robert E. *Christians Rejoice: A Biblical Theology of New Testament Joy.* Fribourg: St. Paul's, 1963.

Barron, Robert. "Unfolding the Divine Plan: Stephen Colbert, J.R.R. Tolkien, John Henry Newman and the Providence of God," *The Tidings* (August 28, 2015) 13.

Barth, Karl. *Epistle to the Philippians.* Translated by James W. Leitch. Richmond: Westminster John Knox, 2002.

Baum, Gregory. *Man Becoming.* New York: Herder and Herder, 1970.

Beardslee, William A. "Saving One's Life By Losing It." *Journal of the American Academy of Religion* 47:1 (March 1979) 57–72.

Beare, Francis Wright. *The Epistle to the Philippians.* San Francisco: Harper & Row, 1959.

Belleville, Linda L. "'Imitate Me, Just as I Imitate Christ': Discipleship in the Corinthian Correspondence." In *Patterns of Discipleship in the New Testament*, edited by R. N. Longenecker, 120–142. Grand Rapids: Eerdmans, 1996.

Betz, Otto. "Jesus and Isaiah 53." In *Jesus and the Suffering Servant: Isaiah 53 and Christian Origins*, edited by William H. Bellinger and William R. Farmer, 70–87. Harrisburg: Trinity, 1998.

Birmingham Oratory. "Tolkein and the Oratory." Accessed November 9, 2016. http://www.birminghamoratory.org.uk/about-the-oratory/tolkein-the-oratory/.

Biviano, Erin Lothes. *The Paradox of Christian Sacrifice: The Loss of Self, The Gift of Self.* New York: Crossroad, 2007.

Bloomquist, L. Gregory. *The Function of Suffering in Philippians.* Sheffield: Journal for the Study of the New Testament, 1993.

———. "Subverted by Joy: Suffering and Joy in Paul's Letter to the Philippians." *Interpretation* 61 no. 3 (July 2007) 270–282.

Bockmuehl, Markus. *The Epistle to the Philippians.* Black's New Testament Commentaries, vol. 11. Peabody, MA: Hendrickson, 1998.

———. "'The Form of God' (Phil. 2:6): Variations on a Theme of Jewish Mysticism." *Journal of Theological Studies* 48 no.1 (1997) 1–23.

Bonhoeffer, Dietrich. *Conspiracy and Imprisonment: 1940–1945*. Edited by Mark S. Brocker. Dietrich Bonhoeffer Works, vol. 16. Minneapolis: Fortress, 2006.

———. *Discipleship*. Edited by John D. Godsey and Geffrey B. Kelly, translated by Barbara Green and Reinhard Krauss. Dietrich Bonhoeffer Works, vol. 4. Minneapolis: Fortress, 2003.

Brant, Jo-Ann A. "The Place of *Mimēsis* in Paul's Thought." *Studies in Religion* 22 (1993) 285–300.

Brondos, David A. *Paul on the Cross: Reconstructing the Apostle's Story of Redemption*. Minneapolis: Fortress, 2006.

Brother Lawrence of the Resurrection, *The Practice of the Presence of God*. Translated by Salvatore Sciurba. Washington, D.C.: ICS, 1994.

Brown, Colin. "Ernst Lohmeyer's *Kyrios Jesus*." In *Where Christology Began: Essays on Philippians 2*, edited by Ralph P. Martin and Brian J. Dodd, 6–42. Louisville: Westminster John Knox, 1998.

Brown, Raphael, trans. *The Little Flowers of Saint Francis*. New York: Image, 1958.

Brown, Raymond E. *The Anchor Bible, The Gospel According to John*. 2 vols. New York: Doubleday, 1966.

———. *The Critical Meaning of the Bible*. New York: Paulist, 1981.

Calhoun, Lawrence G., and Richard G. Tedeschi. *Facilitating Posttraumatic Growth: A Clinician's Guide*. Mahwah: Lawrence Erlbaum, 1999.

———. "The Foundations of Posttraumatic Growth: New Considerations," *Psychological Inquiry*, vol. 15, no. 1 (2004) 93–102.

Castelli, Elizabeth A. *Imitating Paul: A Discourse of Power*. Louisville, KY: Westminster/John Knox, 1991.

Catechism of the Catholic Church. 2nd ed. Citta del Vaticano: Libreria Editrice Vaticana, 1994.

Clarke, Andrew D. "'Be Imitators of Me': Paul's Model of Leadership." *Tyndale Bulletin* 49 no. 2 (1998) 329–360.

Conzelmann, Hans. "χαίρω, χαρά, συγχαίρω." In *Theological Dictionary of the New Testament*, edited by Gerhard Friedrich and translated by Geoffrey W. Bromily 359–376. Vol. 9 of 10. Grand Rapids: William B. Eerdmans, 1974.

Copan, Victor A. "*Mathetes* and *Mimetes*: Exploring an Entangled Relationship." *Bulletin for Biblical Research* 17.2 (2007) 313–323.

———. *Saint Paul as Spiritual Director: An Analysis of the Imitation of Paul with Implications and Applications to the Practice of Spiritual Direction*. Milton Keynes, UK: Paternoster, 2007.

Cousar, Charles B. *Philippians and Philemon: A Commentary*. Louisville: Westminster John Knox, 2009.

———. *Theology of the Cross: The Death of Jesus in the Pauline Letters*. Minneapolis: Fortress, 1990.

Culpepper, R. Alan. "Co-Workers in Suffering: Philippians 2:19–30." *Review & Expositor* 77 no. 3 (1980) 349–358.

De Boer, William P. *The Imitation of Paul: An Exegetical Study*. Kampen: Kok Pharos, 1962.

De Caussade, Jean Pierre. *Self-Abandonment to Divine Providence*. Rockford: Tan, 1959.

Delling, Gerhard. "τέλος, τελέω, ἐπιτελέω." In *Theological Dictionary of the New Testament*, edited by Gerhard Friedrich and translated by Geoffrey W. Bromily, 49–87. Vol. 8 of 10. Grand Rapids: William B. Eerdmans, 1972.

Derrett, Duncan M. "Taking Up the Cross and Turning the Cheek." In *Alternative Approaches to New Testament Study*, 61–78. London: SPCK, 1985.

Dodd, Brian J. "The Story of Christ and the Imitation of Paul in Philippians 2–3." In *Where Christology Began: Essays on Philippians 2*, edited by Ralph P. Martin and Brian J. Dodd, 154–161. Louisville, KY: Westminster John Knox, 1998.

Dodd, C.H. *The Interpretation of the Fourth Gospel*. Cambridge: Cambridge University Press, 1980.

Donahue, John R. *The Theology and Setting of Discipleship in the Gospel of Mark*. Milwaukee: Marquette University Press, 1983.

Donahue, John R. and Daniel J. Harrington. *The Gospel of Mark*. Sacra Pagina, vol. 2. Collegeville: Liturgical, 2002.

Downey, Michael. *Understanding Christian Spirituality*. New York: Paulist, 1997.

Dulles, Avery. *Models of Revelation*. New York: Doubleday, 1983.

Dunn, James D.G. "Christ, Adam, and Prexistence." In *Where Christology Began: Essays on Philippians 2*, edited by Ralph P. Martin and Brian J. Dodd, 74–83. Louisville: Westminster John Knox, 1998.

Ehrensperger, Kathy. "'Be Imitators of Me As I Am of Christ:' A Hidden Discourse on Power and Domination in Paul?" *Lexington Theological Quarterly* 38/4 (2003) 241–261.

Evans, C. Stephen. "Kenotic Christology and the Nature of God." In *Exploring Kenotic Christology*, edited by C. Stephen Evans, 190–217. Oxford: Oxford University Press, 2006.

Evans, Craig A. "Listening for Echoes of Interpreted Scripture." In *Paul and the Scriptures of Israel*, edited by Craig A. Evans and James A. Sanders, 47–51. Sheffield: JSOT, 1993.

Fee, Gordon D. *The First Epistle to the Corinthians*. Grand Rapids: Eerdmans, 1987.

———. "The New Testament and Kenosis Christology." In *Exploring Kenotic Christology*, edited by C. Stephen Evans, 25–44. Oxford: Oxford University Press, 2006.

———. *Paul's Letter to the Philippians*. Grand Rapids: Eerdmans, 1995.

Fischer, James A. "Pauline Literary Forms and Thought Patterns." *Catholic Biblical Quarterly* 39 no. 2 (April 1977) 209–223.

Fishbane, Michael. "The Inwardness of Joy in Jewish Spirituality." In *In Pursuit of Happiness*, edited by Leroy S. Rouner, 71–88. Notre Dame: University of Notre Dame Press, 1995.

Fisk, Bruce N. "The Odyssey of Christ: A Novel Context for Philippians 2:6–11." In *Exploring Kenotic Christology*, edited by C. Stephen Evans, 45–73. Oxford: Oxford University Press, 2006.

Fitzmyer, Joseph A. "The Aramaic Background of Philippians 2:6–11." *Catholic Biblical Quarterly* 50 (1988) 470–483.

Flannery, Austin, ed. *Vatican Council II: Constitutions, Decrees, Declarations*. Northport, NY: Costello, 1996.

Fowl, Stephen. "Christology and Ethics in Philippians 2:5–11." In *Where Christology Began: Essays on Philippians 2*, edited by Ralph P. Martin and Brian J. Dodd, 140–153. Louisville, KY: Westminster John Knox, 1998.

———. "Who's Characterizing Whom and the Difference This Makes: Locating and Centering Paul." In *Society of Biblical Literature* 1993 *Seminar Papers*, 537–553. Missoula: Scholars' Press, 1993.

Fredrickson, David E. "Envious Enemies of the Cross of Christ (Philippians 3:18)." *Word & World* vol. 28. no. 1 (2008) 22–28.

Fretheim, Terence E. *The Suffering of God*. Philadephia: Fortress, 1984.

Gallagher, Timothy M. *The Discernment of Spirits: An Ignatian Guide for Everyday Living*. New York: Crossroad, 2005.

Gianotti, Charles R. "The Meaning of the Divine Name YHWH." *Bibliotheca Sacra* (Jan/Mar 1985) 38–51.

Gibbs, John G. "The Relation Between Creation and Redemption According to Philippians 2:5–11." *Novum Testamentum* 12 no. 3 (July 1970) 270–283.

Glasson, T. Francis. "Two Notes on the Philippians Hymn (II. 6–11)." *New Testament Studies* 21 no. 1 (1974) 133–139.

Goldingay, John. *The Message of Isaiah 40–55: A Literary-Theological Commentary*. London: T&T Clark, 2005.

Gorman, Michael J. *Cruciformity: Paul's Narrative Spirituality of the Cross*. Grand Rapids: William B. Eerdmans, 2001.

———. *Inhabiting the Cruciform God: Kenosis, Justification, and Theosis in Paul's Narrative Soteriology*. Grand Rapids: William B. Eerdmans, 2009.

Green, Donald E. "The Folly of the Cross." *Master's Seminary Journal* 15 no. 1 (Spring 2004) 59–69.

Green, William Scott. "Doing the Text's Work For It: Richard Hays on Paul's Use of Scripture." In *Paul and the Scriptures of Israel*, edited by Craig A. Evans and James A. Sanders, 58–63. Sheffield: JSOT, 1993.

Gregory of Nyssa. *Commentary on the Song of Songs*. Brookline: Hellenic College Press, 1987.

Griffiths, J. Gwyn. "The Disciple's Cross." *New Testament Studies* 16 (July 1970) 358–364.

Hansen, G. Walter. *The Letter to the Philippians*. Grand Rapids: William B. Eerdmans, 2009.

Hanson, Anthony Tyrrell. *The Paradox of the Cross in the Thought of St. Paul*. JSNT Sup. 17; Sheffield: JSOT, 1987.

Harvey, Dorthea Ward. "Joy." In *The Interpreter's Dictionary of the Bible*, edited by George Authur Buttrick, 2:1000–1001. New York: Abingdon, 1962.

Hawthorne, Gerald F. "The Imitation of Christ: Discipleship in Philippians." In *Patterns of Discipleship in the New Testament*, edited by R. N. Longenecker, 163–179. Grand Rapids: Eerdmans, 1996.

———. "In the Form of God and Equal with God (Philippians 2:6)." In *Where Christology Began: Essays on Philippians 2*, edited by Ralph P. Martin and Brian J. Dodd, 96–110. Louisville, KY: Westminster John Knox, 1998.

———. *Philippians*. World Biblical Commentary, vol. 43. Waco: Word, 1983.

Hays, Richard B. *The Conversion of the Imagination: Paul as Interpreter of Israel's Scripture*. Grand Rapids: William B. Eerdmans, 2005.

———. *Echoes of Scripture in the Letters of Paul*. New Haven: Yale University Press, 1989.

Hogan, Laura. "A Pauline Theology of Suffering, Transformation and Joy as Found in Philippians." MA thesis, St. John's Seminary, Camarillo, California (2011).

The Holy Bible, New International Version. Grand Rapids: Zondervan, 2011.

The Holy See. "Mother Teresa of Calcutta (1910–1997)." Accessed November 9, 2016. http://www.vatican.va/news_services/liturgy/saints/ns_lit_doc_20031019_madre-teresa_en.html.

Hooker, Morna D. *From Adam to Christ: Essays on Paul*. Cambridge: Cambridge University Press, 1990.

Hoover, Roy W. "The Harpagmos Enigma: A Philological Solution," *Harvard Theological Review* 64 (1971) 95–119.

Howard, George. "Philippians 2:6–11 and the Human Christ." *Catholic Biblical Quarterly* 40 no. 3 (July 1978) 368–387.

Hubbard, Moyer V. *New Creation in Pauline Letters and Thought.* Cambridge: Cambridge University Press, 2002.

Hurtado, Larry W. "Jesus as Lordly Example in Philippians 2:5–11," In *From Jesus to Paul,* 113–126. Waterloo, Ontario: Wilfrid Laurier University Press, 1984.

John of the Cross. *The Dark Night.* In *The Collected Works of St. John of the Cross,* translated by Kieran Kavanaugh and Otilio Rodriguez, 353–457. Washington: ICS, 1991.

———. *The Spiritual Canticle.* In *The Collected Works of St. John of the Cross,* translated by Kieran Kavanaugh and Otilio Rodriguez, 461–630. Washington: ICS, 1991.

John Paul II. Encyclical Letter *Fides et Ratio.* September 15, 1998.

Julian of Norwich, *A Book of Showings to the Anchoress Julian of Norwich,* part 2, edited by Edmund Colledge and James Walsh. Toronto: Pontifical Institute of Mediaeval Studies, 1978.

———. *Showings.* Translated by Edmund Colledge and James Walsh. New York: Paulist Press, 1978.

Käsemann, Ernst. "A Critical Analysis of Philippians 2:5–11." Translated by A.F. Carse. *Journal for Theology and Church* 5 (1968) 45–88.

Kilcourse, George. "Breath, Breathing." In *The New Dictionary of Catholic Spirituality,* edited by Michael Downey, 105–106. Collegeville: Liturgical, 1993.

Kington, Tom. "Mother Teresa Declared a Saint as Pope Francis Lauds Her in Vatican Ceremony." *Los Angeles Times* (September 4, 2016). http://www.latimes.com/world/la-fg-mother-teresa-canonization-20160903-snap-story.html.

Kitamori, Kazoh. *Theology of the Pain of God.* Eugene, OR: Wipf & Stock, 2005.

Kozar, Joseph Vlcek. "Absent Joy: An Investigation of the Narrative Pattern of Repetition and Variation in the Parables of Luke 15." *Toronto Journal of Theology,* vol. 8, no. 1 (Spring 1992) 82–94.

Kreitzer, Larry J. "'When At Last He Is First!' Philippians 2:9–11 and the Exaltation of the Lord." In *Where Christology Began: Essays on Philippians* 2, edited by Ralph P. Martin and Brian J. Dodd, 111–127. Louisville, KY: Westminster John Knox, 1998.

Kurz, W. S. "Kenotic Imitation of Paul and of Christ in Philippians 2 and 3." In *Discipleship in the New Testament,* edited by F.F. Segovia, 103–126. Philadelphia: Fortress, 1985.

Laird, Martin. *Gregory of Nyssa and the Grasp of Faith.* Oxford: Oxford University Press, 2004.

Langis, Dean. "Joy: A Scriptural and Patristic Understanding." *Greek Orthodox Theological Review,* vol. 35, no. 1 (1990) 47–57.

Latourelle, Rene. *Theology of Revelation.* New York: Alba House, 1987.

Lemmel, Helen H., composer. "Turn Your Eyes Upon Jesus" (1922). Timeless Truths Online Library. Accessed November 9, 2016. http://library.timelesstruths.org/music/Turn_Your_Eyes_upon_Jesus/.

Lightfoot, J.B. *St. Paul's Epistle to the Philippians.* London: MacMillan, 1894.

Linahan, Jane E. "Kenosis: Metaphor of Relationship," In *Theology and Conversation: Towards a Relational Theology,* edited by J. Haers and P. De Mey, 299–309. Louvain: Leuven University Press, 2003.

Longenecker, R. N., ed. *Patterns of Discipleship in the New Testament.* Grand Rapids: Eerdmans, 1996.

Louth, Andrew. *The Origins of the Christian Mystical Tradition: From Plato to Denys.* Oxford: Clarendon, 1981.

Lovell, Joel. "The Late, Great Stephen Colbert." *Gentleman's Quarterly* (August 17, 2015). http://www.gq.com/story/stephen-colbert-gq-cover-story.

Malcolm, Lois. "The Wisdom of the Cross." In *Reason and the Reasons of Faith,* edited by Paul J. Griffiths and Reinhard Hütter. New York: T & T Clark, 2005.

Malina, Bruce J. "'Let Him Deny Himself' (Mark 8:34 & Par): A Social Psychological Model Self-Denial." *Biblical Theology Bulletin* 24 (1994) 106–119.

Marchal, Joseph A. *Hierarchy, Unity, and Imitation: A Feminist Rhetorical Analysis of Power Dynamics in Paul's Letter to the Philippians.* Atlanta: Society of Biblical Literature, 2006.

Martin, Ralph P. *Carmen Christi: Philippians 2:5–11 in Recent Interpretation and in the Setting of Early Christian Worship.* Cambridge: Cambridge University Press, 1967.

———. *The New Century Bible Commentary: Philippians.* Grand Rapids: William B. Eerdmans, 1982.

Martin, Ralph P. and Brian J. Dodd, eds. *Where Christology Began: Essays on Philippians 2.* Louisville, KY: Westminster John Knox, 1998.

Mays, James L. "Mark 8:27—9:1," *Interpretation* 30 (1976) 174–178.

McClain, Alva J. "The Doctrine of Kenosis in Philippians 2:5–8." *Master's Seminary Journal* 9 no. 1 (Spring 1998) 85–96.

McGinn, Bernard. *The Foundations of Mysticism: Origins to the Fifth Century.* New York: Crossroad, 1991.

Michaelis, W. "μιμέομαι, μιμητής, συμμιμητής." In *Theological Dictionary of the New Testament,* edited by Gerhard Kittel and translated by Geoffrey W. Bromily, 659–674. Vol. 4 of 10. Grand Rapids: William B. Eerdmans, 1967.

Milbank, John. "Can a Gift Be Given: Prolegomena to a Future Trinitarian Metaphysic." In *Rethinking Metaphysics,* edited by L. Gregory Jones and Stephen E. Fowl, 119–161. Oxford: Blackwell, 1995.

Mother Teresa. *Come Be My Light: The Private Writings of the 'Saint of Calcutta',* edited by Brian Kolodiejchuk. New York: Image, 2007.

Moloney, Francis J. *The Gospel of John.* Edited by Daniel J. Harrington. Sacra Pagina, vol. 4. Collegeville: Liturgical Press, 1988.

Moorcroft, Jennifer. *He Is My Heaven: The Life of Elizabeth of the Trinity.* Washington, D.C.: ICS, 2001.

Murphy-O Connor, Jerome. "'Even death on a cross': Crucifixion in the Pauline Letters," In *The Cross in Christian Tradition,* edited by Elizabeth A. Dreyer, 21–50. New York: Paulist, 2000.

———. *Paul: His Story.* Oxford: Oxford University Press, 2004.

New American Bible. New York: Catholic Book Publishing, 1991.

Newport, Frank. "Mother Teresa Voted by American People as Most Admired Person of the Century." Gallup News Service (Dec. 31, 1999). http://www.gallup.com/poll/3367/mother-teresa-voted-american-people-most-admired-person-century.aspx.

Noffke, Suzanne. "Soul." In *The New Dictionary of Catholic Spirituality,* edited by Michael Downey, 908–910. Collegeville: Liturgical, 1993.

Origen. *The Song of Songs, Commentary and Homilies.* Translated and annotated by R.P. Lawson. New York: Paulist, 1956.

O'Rourke, et al, "Measuring Post-traumatic Changes in Spirituality/Religiosity," *Mental Health, Religion and Culture* (June 2008) 1–10.

Osiek, Carolyn. *Philippians, Philemon.* Abingdon New Testament Commentaries. Nashville: Abingdon, 2000.

Park, M. Sydney. *Submission Within the Godhead and the Church in the Epistle to the Philippians.* London: T&T Clark, 2007.

Peerbolte, Bert-Jan Lietaert. "The Name Above All Names (Philippians 2:9)." In *The Revelation of the Name YHWH to Moses: Perspectives from Judaism, the Pagan Graeco-Roman World, and Early Christianity,* edited by George H. van Kooten, 187–206. Leiden: Brill, 2006.

Plank, Karl A. *Paul and the Irony of Affliction.* Atlanta: Scholars' Press, 1987.

Polkinghorne, John, ed. *The Work of Love: Creation as Kenosis.* Grand Rapids, MI: William B. Eerdmans, 2001.

Post, Stephen G. "The Inadequacy of Selflessness: God's Suffering and the Theory of Love." *Journal of the American Academy of Religion* 56:2 (1988) 213–228.

Power, David N. *Love Without Calculation: A Reflection on Divine Kenosis.* New York: Crossroad, 2005.

Powers, Jessica. "Beauty, Too, Seeks Surrender." In *The Selected Poetry of Jessica Powers,* 72. Washington, DC: ICS, 1999.

Proudfoot, C. Merrill. "Imitation or Realistic Participation? A Study of Paul's Concept of 'Suffering With Christ.'" *Interpretation* 17 no. 2 (April 1963) 140–160.

Rahner, Karl. *Foundations of Christian Faith.* New York: Crossroad, 1978.

Reid, Jennings B. *Jesus: God's Emptiness, God's Fullness: The Christology of St. Paul.* New York: Paulist, 1990.

Rendon, Jim. "Post-Traumatic Stress's Surprisingly Positive Flip Side." *New York Times* (March 22, 2012). http://www.nytimes.com/2012/03/25/magazine/post-traumatic-stresss-surprisingly-positive-flip-side.html?pagewanted=all.

Rhoads, David. "Losing Life for Others in the Face of Death: Mark's Standards of Judgment." *Interpretation* 47 (1993) 358–369.

Richard, Lucien J. *A Kenotic Christology.* Boston: University Press of America, 1982.

Robertson, A.T. *Paul's Joy in Christ: Studies in Philippians.* Edited by W.C. Strickland. Revised ed. Nashville: Broadman, 1959.

Rofé, Alexander. "How Is the Word Fulfilled? Isaiah 55:6–11 Within the Theological Debate of Its Time." In *Canon, Theology, and Old Testament Interpretation,* edited by Gene M. Tucker, David L. Petersen and Robert R. Wilson, 246–261. Philadelphia: Fortress, 1988.

Sanders, Boykin. "Imitating Paul: 1 Cor 4:16." *Harvard Theological Review* 74 no. 4 (October 1981) 353–363.

Sanders, Jack T. *The New Testament Christological Hymns: Their Historical Religious Background.* Cambridge: Cambridge University Press, 1971.

Sanderson, Brandon. *Alcatraz Versus the Evil Librarians.* New York: Scholastic, 2007.

Savage, Timothy B. *Power Through Weakness: Paul's Understanding of the Christian Ministry in 2 Corinthians.* Cambridge: Cambridge University Press, 1996.

Seccombe, David P. "Take Up Your Cross." In *God Who Is Rich in Mercy: Essays Presented to Dr. D.B. Knox,* 139–151. Homebush, Australia: Lancer, 1986.

Second Vatican Ecumenical Council, "Dogmatic Constitution on Divine Revelation, *Dei Verbum.*" In *Vatican Council II: Constitutions, Decrees, Declarations,* edited by Austin Flannery, 97–115. Northport, NY: Costello, 1996.

Segal, Alan F. *Paul the Convert: The Apostolate and Apostasy of Saul the Pharisee*. New Haven: Yale University Press, 1990.

Silva, Moisés. *Philippians*. Baker Exegetical Commentary on the New Testament. 2nd ed. Grand Rapids: Baker Academic, 2005.

Skinner, Matthew L. "Denying Self, Bearing a Cross, and Following Jesus: Unpacking the Imperatives of Mark 8:34" *Word & World* 23:3 (Summer 2003) 321–331.

Smyth, Bernard T. *Paul: Mystic and Missionary*. New York: Orbis, 1980.

Spink, Kathryn. *Mother Teresa: An Authorized Biography*. New York: HarperCollins 2011.

Spoto, Donald. *Reluctant Saint: The Life of Francis of Assisi*. New York: Penguin Compass, 2002.

Standhartinger, Angela. "'Join in Imitating Me' (Philippians 3.17): Towards an Interpretation of Philippians 3." *New Testament Studies* 54 (2008) 417–435.

Strauss, Neil. "The Subversive Joy of Stephen Colbert." *Rolling Stone* (September 17, 2009). http://www.rollingstone.com/movies/news/the-subversive-joy-of-stephen-colbert-20090917.

Talstra, Eep. "The Name in Kings and Chronicles." In *The Revelation of the Name YHWH to Moses: Perspectives from Judaism, the Pagan Graeco-Roman World, and Early Christianity*, edited by George H. van Kooten, 55–70. Leiden: Brill, 2006.

Tedeschi, Richard G., and Lawrence G. Calhoun. "Posttraumatic Growth: Conceptual Foundations and Empirical Evidence," *Psychological Inquiry*, Vol. 15, No. 1 (2004) 1–18.

———. "The Posttraumatic Growth Inventory: Measuring the Positive Legacy of Trauma," *Journal of Traumatic Stress* 9 (1996) 455–471.

Teresa of Avila. *The Interior Castle*. In *The Collected Works of St. Teresa of Avila*, translated by Kieran Kavanaugh and Otilio Rodriguez, vol. 2, 263–452. Washington: ICS, 1980.

———. *Interior Castle*. Translated and edited by E. Allison Peers. New York: Doubleday, 1961.

———. *Meditations on the Song of Songs*. In *The Collected Works of St. Teresa of Avila*, translated by Kieran Kavanaugh and Otilio Rodriguez, vol. 2, 207–260. Washington: ICS, 1980.

Thérèse of Lisieux. *Story of a Soul*. Translated by John Clarke. 3rd ed. Washington, D.C.: ICS, 1996.

———. *The Story of a Soul*. Translated and edited by Robert J. Edmonson. Brewster, Massachusetts: Paraclete, 2006.

Thompson, Thomas R. "Nineteenth Century Kenotic Christology: The Waxing, Waning, and Weighing of a Quest for a Coherent Orthodoxy." In *Exploring Kenotic Christology: The Self-Emptying of God*, edited by C. Stephen Evans, 74–111. Oxford: Oxford University Press 2006.

Thurston, Bonnie Bowman, et al. *Philippians and Philemon*. Sacra Pagina Series. Collegeville: Liturgical, 2005.

UNC School of Medicine. "The Grayson Clamp Family Story." UNC Otolaryngology/ Head and Neck Surgery, University of North Carolina at Chapel Hill School of Medicine. Accessed November 9, 2016. http://www.med.unc.edu/ent/grayson-clamp-family-story.

Van Bekkum, Wout Jac. "What's in a Divine Name? Exodus 3 in Biblical and Rabbinic Tradition." In *The Revelation of the Name YHWH to Moses: Perspectives from Judaism, the Pagan Graeco-Roman World, and Early Christianity*, edited by George H. van Kooten, 3–15. Leiden: Brill, 2006.

Van Kooten, George H., ed. *The Revelation of the Name YHWH to Moses: Perspectives from Judaism, the Pagan Graeco-Roman World, and Early Christianity.* Leiden: Brill, 2006.

Von Balthasar, Hans Urs. "Joy and the Cross." In *The Gift of Joy*, edited by Christian Duquoc, 83–96. New York: Paulist, 1968.

Wagner, J. Ross. *Heralds of the Good News: Isaiah and Paul in Concert in the Letter to the Romans.* Leiden: Brill, 2002.

———. "Rejoice in the Lord! Philippians 4:4–9 and Psalm 131." *The Princeton Seminary Bulletin* 28 no. 1 (2007) 1–6.

Ward, Keith. "Cosmos and Kenosis," In *The Work of Love: Creation as Kenosis*, edited by John Polkinghorne, 152–166. Grand Rapids: William B. Eerdmans, 2001.

Webster, John B. "The Imitation of Christ." *Tyndale Bulletin* 37 (1986) 95–120.

Welborn, L.L. *Paul, the Fool of Christ: A Study of 1 Corinthians 1–4 in the Comic-Philosophic Tradition.* New York: T & T Clark, 2005.

Wiseman, James A. "Mysticism." In *The New Dictionary of Catholic Spirituality*, edited by Michael Downey, 681–692. Collegeville: Liturgical, 1993.

Wright, N.T. *The Climax of the Covenant.* Minneapolis: Fortress, 1993.

———. *Paul: In Fresh Perspective.* Edinburgh: Clark/Minneapolis: Fortress, 2005.

Wuest, Kenneth Samuel. "When Jesus Emptied Himself." *Bibliotheca Sacra* 115 no. 458 (April 1958) 153–158.